MEMORIES
OF A
BERLIN
CHILDHOOD

To my friend Lee

with affection

Marianne

Marianne Buchwalter

April 2015

ii

Another commemorative history book published by

Premiere Editions International Inc.
2397 NW Kings Blvd. #311
Corvallis, Oregon 97330-3986
503/752-4239 ❑ FAX 503/752-4463

Printed in the United States of America
Cascade Printing Company, Corvallis, Oregon
Editor: Irene L. Gresick
Designer: Donna Reyes
Front Cover Illustration: Randall Stauss
Back Cover Photo of Author: Josef Castéra

First Edition
Library of Congress Catalog Number: 95-67040
ISBN: 9633818-4-9

AN DIE ERINNERUNG . . .

To the Memory . . .

ACKNOWLEDGMENTS

My family was lucky. With our arrival in America in February, 1939, we had left behind the horrors of war, destruction and annihilation. We were given the chance to start life anew. Yet, fleeting memories of my Berlin childhood, so dramatically different from the early lives my American contemporaries, persisted in knocking at the doors of some inner chamber. In the face of a growing denial of the Holocaust and the notion that Hitler's persecution of the Jews was mere propaganda, the opening of these doors became compelling. The necessity to write this book turned into an all-consuming endeavor, a fascinating journey, with many people cheering me on.

My deep gratitude goes to Sister Helene Brand, a poet and English professor at Oregon's Marylhurst College. At the outset of my journey, she listened patiently to early fragments of the text and made significant suggestions. A.B. Paulson, an English professor at Portland State University, urged me on with his generous assessment of early versions of the manuscript. My deep thanks go to my children for their strong support — to Julie, Nicki, Andy and Kate for their careful readings and editorial comments — to Charlie and Lisa for their enthusiastic feedback — and to Jonathan for introducing me to the world of publishing. John and Joan Shipley, Steffi Posament, E.K. MacColl, Jay Margulies, Anita Witt and the late Hans Fink, MD, gave my text sensitive readings, and Else Lowen and Eva Carr helped me recall details long forgotten. Serendipitous encounters played a considerable part in the completion of the book. Philippa Brunsman streamlined the text, Micaela Grudin was present with joyful support, and Irene Gresick made publishing *Memories of a Berlin Childhood* a reality.

My most profound thankfulness and unending devotion go to my late husband, Fred M. Buchwalter, whose patient, enthusiastic and constant encouragement propelled me through moments of doubt and hesitation.

TABLE OF CONTENTS

PROLOGUE

Quickly, before my memories fade — become hazy, imprecise — I must recount my first fourteen years. In and out of cloudy reminiscence, they surface with luminous clarity. From Oregon, the place I now call home, the shape and flavor of another, earlier landscape peopled with old, familiar faces reappear in dreams and at unexpected moments in everyday life.

Yes, I had a life before Hitler. That life was not an unusual or a remarkable one. Yet, over the years, it has become transformed into a life filled with enchantment and harmony against a backdrop of a disintegrating society and interspersed with the unavoidable pains of growing up. My parents did not belong to the intellectual, cultural or political elite of Berlin. They did not join causes. They did not take strong positions. They did not stand out. They were part of a solid, conservative, law-abiding citizenry, participating spectators, rather than actors in the drama of the theater called Berlin.

Rome, London, Paris and many other European cities, were over a thousand years old when Berlin, a newcomer on the rivers Spree and Havel, was founded

in 1237. An open city, it welcomed people generously
from all parts of Europe. Its liberalism created a haven
for the persecuted, the dissatisfied, the adventurous.
They came from east, west, north and south, and helped
found a metropolis whose intellectual vibrancy, economic
vitality and cultural vigor became unique in western
Europe. To inhabitants and visitors alike, Berlin in the
1920s and early 30s was *Die schoenste Stadt der Welt*, the
most beautiful city in the world.

Indeed, Berlin was a showplace of imposing
boulevards and meticulously maintained old buildings,
with parks, lakes and rivers. It was a playground for rich
and poor, young and old. Its cultural life with
outstanding opera, symphony orchestras and theater was
beyond compare. Its population was renowned for
individuality and outspokenness — *Berliners Fresse* — a
raucous, humorous and saucy tongue.

Then, in 1933, Adolf Hitler became Chancellor. The
mood of the city turned bitter. The spontaneous and
unselfconscious joy faded away. Its lighthearted song was
silenced. I was nine years old.

BRANDENBURGISCHE STRASSE, CIRCA 1938.
COURTESY OF JOHN SHIPLEY

CHAPTER 1
THE BARONESS

November 10, 1938. The doorbell rings urgently. In sweeps the Baroness, her hair even wilder than usual. Wisps escape from her loosely fastened chignon and flutter around her forehead and cheeks. "Where is Julian?" she asks. When told that he's not home, she is relieved. "He

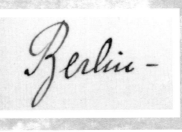

absolutely must stay away from the flat. He must not be seen," she cries out. We already know the Gestapo is looking for my father, but her quavering voice, normally so strong, intensifies my terror.

My mother, my aunt, my little brother Hans, and I huddle in our small apartment on Konstanzer Strasse. My mother, who rarely shows her feelings, sits as if paralyzed while Tante Toni hovers around her with cups of hot tea. My brother and I are scared. We don't know what to do.

Early this morning, a phone call from a non-Jewish friend high in government circles informs us that during the night, in Berlin as throughout Germany, Synagogues have been burned, Jewish-owned store windows smashed and residences ransacked. Jewish men were forced out of their apartments at gun point and delivered to police headquarters and concentration camps. My father must disappear, go into hiding.

It was too soon for us to realize that we had innocently slept through the night of terror that was to become known to the world as *Kristallnacht*, the night of broken glass.

"I was just walking the dogs by your old apartment," the Baroness continues, "when the manager ran after me, breathless and shaken. Two Gestapo men inquired as to where Julian was; but all she told them was that he had moved."

Thank God for old Frau Zeck! She has not given away our new address. She always liked our family, especially my father. With his ever-courteous and cheery manner and his daily friendly greetings bordering on the flirtatious, he is able to coax from her grouchy and wrinkled face a coy blush. She turns away with a giggle. "But Herr Schybilski, you must not tease an old woman like me."

With the help of the Baroness's connections as an interior decorator, we had found our temporary quarters on Konstanzer Strasse. In early October of 1938, we vacated the apartment where I lived eight of my fourteen years. All our furniture and belongings had been packed and shipped to the United States. Within weeks, upon receipt of our American visa, we are to follow.

Ideally, nothing stands in the way of our leaving. My father has been fortunate to find a buyer for his factory, and on October first an unexpected letter from Herr Zorn, the rector of the Hohenzollern Lyzeum informs my parents that I, Marianne Valli Schybilski, student in the *Unter Terzia*, the fourth year of high school, need not return. I am no longer welcome. I was kicked out.

"Well, now, where is Julian?" asks the Baroness, sitting down on a couch that sags in the middle and, like all the rest of the furniture in that cheerless place, gives off a musty odor. My mother, made more lively by the Baroness's presence, reports that my father is out riding the Berlin subways so as not to be picked up by the Nazis. "I don't have the slightest idea when Julchen will be back," she says. "Nor do I know where he is. If only he would call!"

"He'll be all right." The Baroness's optimism leaves no doubt. "From the moment I met him, I knew that here was a man guided by a lucky star."

My parents had met the Baroness von Ameluxen in 1936 on a winter vacation in Switzerland and became close friends. Much to everyone's surprise, it turned out that we lived only two blocks apart, on Brandenburgische Strasse.

Like a fairy queen, she entered my life. Every one of her visits became a special event. In keeping with our household motto that *children should be seen but not heard*, I watched from a far corner in speechless fascination. Her every move registered grace and strength. Unlike my mother who seemed frightened of bright colors, the Baroness splashed them indiscriminately onto her person with true zest. Shimmering suits and gowns in flamboyant colors of magenta, purple or dark amber draped her imposing figure while heavy brooches and clasps, that I so far had only spotted in museums, valiantly held up her hair.

"Tonight I have superb seats for the Opera!" She used to thrust her long white gloves on the settee at the entry door and sail into our living room for a quick Sherry before my father escorted her and my mother to Kempinski for dinner.

I developed an immediate girlhood crush on this elegant, vivacious woman who seemed to me to hail from a world of luxury and mystery, so different from our family's uneventful existence. Unfailingly she listens to me with attention, and today, pats my shoulder reassuringly, yet without show of sentimentality.

My first visit to her apartment was when I was eleven years old. Never before had I seen such a tasteful place. The Baroness occupied a penthouse, where large, stiff old-fashioned portraits, no doubt of family members, contrasted with strange and colorful paintings. My parents later told me they were by painters called Klee, Nolde and Kandinsky, names unfamiliar to me then.

Couches and armchairs upholstered in off-white woven fabric set off the oriental carpets and the polished oak floor. White flowers were arranged on the furniture, and large plants filled the corners of the room. What luxury and comfort! I, too, would be an interior decorator some day.

Two miniature poodles jumped up on me when Hilde, the maid, showed me into the living room. The Baroness appeared, dressed in a long ruby-red gown, her auburn hair's usual chaos tamed by prominent tortoise shell combs. She embraced me, bid me sit next to her on one of her lavish couches and asked me about school, my friends and my hobbies. "When you are with your parents, you're always so quiet."

From a silver box, she offered me candies with shiny wrappings and I proceeded to tell her about Reni and

Elisabeth, my two best friends, about Fräulein Müller, my favorite teacher and about Erika and Christine who did not like me because I was Jewish.

I felt deliciously grown up. Her warmth made me expansive. I poured out to her my love for poetry, for the French language and for writers like Balzac and Flaubert, with whom I had just become acquainted.

"You must read *Anna Karenina*," said the Baroness. "I was exactly your age when I first read it. You'll love it." Being with her was just like being with someone my age, only better because she knew so much.

She sensed my disappointment when she had to end our visit. "You must come again, Marianne. We'll have lots to talk about and I'll show you the rest of my apartment." Gently she stroked my cheek. "You'll grow up to be very beautiful. You'll never have a shortage of admirers."

What was she saying? I considered myself absolutely ugly, unsightly, with a mouth like a metal trap whenever I spoke or smiled. But even my flamboyant and handsome orthodontist, Dr. Wongschovski, predicted a romantic future after my dental transformation was completed. As he peered into my mouthful of braces, his impeccable, starched shirts crushing against me and his fragrant hair pomade filling my nostrils, he promised to take me dining and dancing once I was older. I wondered, did he spin this yarn for all his young female patients?

Yet, such frivolous thoughts are far from my mind on this November afternoon, as we pass the time chatting with the Baroness. I am dispatched to buy an almond coffee ring at the bakery down the street. Eating cake and drinking coffee with our optimistic and expansive friend, we talk about the sadness of leaving behind a life of comfort and certainty. Tante Toni's departure date is still uncertain. Her son, Fritz, who left for America in 1935, has yet to mail her the necessary affidavit. It should arrive any day now.

Our own affidavit arrived some time ago from Onkel Herman, my mother's brother. This important document guaranteed that we would not become burdens to the United States government.

People called Onkel Herman lucky. But more than anything, he was alert and seized opportunities that came his way. The Baroness has heard Onkel Herman's story before, but perhaps to divert us, she insists on hearing it again. My mother recounts how my uncle decided to leave Germany in 1933 when, in a newsreel, he saw Nazis in goosestep marching down the streets of Munich and Berlin. "This place scares me, I will not stay," he had argued with my father who considered himself a good Jew and a good German. Just like Onkel Herman, my father had fought in the First World War, and had been awarded the Iron Cross for bravery in action. For him, the idea of leaving Germany was unthinkable. "This man Hitler is crazy. The Germans won't tolerate him. He won't last."

One day, Onkel Herman happened upon a small notice in the *Frankfurt Zeitung* stating that a certain Mr. Hummel in Portland, Oregon, USA, searched for someone in Germany to exchange properties with him. A strong sympathy for Hitler's ideologies summoned him back to the land of his German forefathers.

My enterprising and adventurous Onkel Herman traveled to Oregon, where, to his great surprise, he found that an equitable exchange could be arranged. The two families lived in comparable two-story private homes, in pleasant neighborhoods with well-kept gardens, and a car in each garage. Onkel Herman's brewery experience made him a valuable commodity and he soon found employment.

Curtains remained on windows, furniture and kitchenware were left in place. Only family treasures and personal effects made the voyage across the Atlantic. The year 1935 opened up a new life for both families.

"Probably the best story I ever heard," exclaims the Baroness. "If I didn't trust you implicitly, Erna, I'd think you made it all up. It sounds like a fairy tale."

"It's hard to believe," my mother agrees. "But it's the truth, and soon we, too, hope to land in Oregon." My parents had visited Onkel Herman and his family and now hoped to follow him to Oregon to start a new life.

The street lights now flicker through the darkness outside. The wind whips the leaves off trees. People make their way home at the day's end.

"I must go," says the Baroness, reaching for her coat. "Keep me posted and call me immediately when you have news of Julian. But remember, I know he is safe!"

I hope she is right. I want to believe her. My brother and I accompany her part way along Brandenburgische Strasse, and by our favorite confectionery store, Erich Hamann, whose marzipan potatoes and window displays of chocolates and pralines, especially at holiday time, are unforgettable. With pfennigs from my meager allowance, I occasionally treat myself to the marzipan or the coconut flakes that come in mixed colors of pink, white and brown. The small paper sacks embossed with pink and gold flowers, into which the saleswoman drops my modest purchases, become keepsakes tucked away in one of my dresser drawers.

The familiar streets, now empty, appear eerie. We see no one we know. Our residential, tree-covered neighborhood shows no sign of destruction, no broken glass. Obviously, none of the neighborhood stores have Jewish owners. For once, the presence of my little brother with his navy-blue wool coat and matching French beret at my side, searching for my hand, makes me feel needed and protective and protected as well. Surely, no one would harm two children.

On our way home, we stop at the small delicatessen at the corner of Brandenburgische and Düsseldorfer Strasse, where I was to buy cold cuts for supper. Its owner is nicknamed *der kleine Mann* (the little man), because next to his hefty wife, and among his huge array of salamis, hams, salads and smoked and pickled fish, he looks so insignificant, so minuscule. Hams and sausages hang against the rear wall. *Blutwurst, Mettwurst, Thuringer,* Italian and Hungarian salamis, neatly arranged behind a glass counter, are feasts for sight and smell.

"How are your parents?" he asks with a searching look. "Are they all right?"

The genuine concern in his voice touches me. I could only shrug my shoulder. He would understand. He wraps my small purchases of Westphalian ham, Hungarian Salami and two sour *Spreewald* pickles into neat packages, and as usual offers us a bonus slice.

We walk home past our old apartment which in ghostlike emptiness stares out into the chilly November night. Gone are the curtains, the green plants of the winter garden in Tante Toni's room, the balcony's red geraniums, and all the familiar objects of our daily lives. What a far cry our present cramped quarters are from our spacious old flat! Yet, what does it matter, as long as we are safe and my father comes home soon.

The lit streetcars 3 and 44 flash by with their unique hissing sounds, stopping every three or four blocks. Only rarely did I use them. Walking was decreed to be good for me and the streetcar was an expendable luxury.

"Stop staring, Marianne." My brother tugs at my sleeve, yanking me out of my reveries. "I'm cold and I want to go home."

"OK, let's race." We run along the dark streets, dash up the two flights of stairs and arrive at the apartment breathless. My mother and aunt greet us with the news that my father had called.

"Vati is fine," my mother reports. "He says he is exhausted, needs a bath and hopes never to ride another subway. There'll also be a surprise when he gets home late tonight."

Relieved, we escape to our rooms after dinner. The need for comfort has passed. I am glad that Tante Toni spends the night and I think about the day's events. I cannot help but think about the Baroness who holds such fascination for me and about the time she crossed my path unexpectedly.

With the first snowfall early in January that year, Liselotte, a classmate, phoned to announce that she would be over soon to plan a ski outing to the Grunewald. The two of us had struck up a friendship when we discovered our shared love for skiing. Much to my amazement she had no scruples about visiting the home of a Jewish girl. Maybe her parents were not Nazis.

I was not particularly pleased that Anna had answered the door to show her to my room. What would Liselotte think about us having a maid and an apartment that may strike her as large and extravagant. Never having been to her apartment or, for that matter, to the homes of any of my gentile classmates, I had no idea how they lived. Our sizable living and dining rooms, the long corridors with doors that opened to five bedrooms and the kitchen with its maids' quarters, must have seemed lavish. Being Jewish was already enough of a difference. I did not relish further disparities.

Yet, Liselotte seemed oblivious to the surroundings. "I couldn't stand being home one more minute. The noise of my sister, her baby and visiting relatives drove me crazy. When shall we go skiing?"

I dreaded introducing visitors to my mother. She had a habit of asking embarrassing and intrusive questions, such as "Where do you live?", "What does your father do?", and "Where did you get your dress?" To avoid such an encounter, I suggested we go for a walk.

Sloshing through heaps of dirty city snow, we made our way down Brandenburgische Strasse to Kurfürstendamm.

Along the way we marveled at the window displays in stores: skirts, sweaters and blouses in Wiener Strickmoden; linens and tablecloths in Grünfeld; crystal, silver and leather things beckoning us seductively in Rosenhain.

We passed crowded cafés that looked warm and cozy with steamed-up windows that hid indefinite shapes of people enveloped in clouds of cigarette smoke. We gazed curiously through the windows of Café Möring and Café Dobrien, the beer hall Mampe and, crossing the street, ended up at the Café Kranzler, at the corner of Joachimsthaler Strasse.

"Have you ever gone into any of these cafés?" asked Liselotte.

"A few times with my mother, but that was long ago." I replied, "My Tante Toni use to take me to a small café on Unter den Linden where she would meet her lady friends. I loved ordering those pastries."

"Come on, let's go in here. I've got some money."

Liselotte had more nerve than I. To go to a café for no special reason seemed frivolous. Such outings had always marked special events, a reward for being good, a birthday,

BERLIN
CIRCA 1930

or a satisfactory report card. My mother considered even the purchase of a lemonade or an ice-cream cone an extravagance, guaranteed to spoil character.

In view of such restraints, small wonder that I agreed only hesitantly to Liselotte's daring suggestion.

We stood at the doors of Kranzler as men and women, mostly in bulky fur coats, came and went. In our little woolen winter coats, knee-high socks and braids to our waists, we presented a striking contrast to the fashionable crowd. The doorman, in a huge gray great-coat and a top hat with a large band imprinted with KRANZLER, viewed us benignly. He gave us a fatherly pat and urged us in out of the cold. We took the plunge and promptly found ourselves enveloped in clouds of smoke and the tantalizing aroma of coffee. A steady hum of voices intermingled with the clatter of dishes, coughs and laughter. We were seated at a small corner table from where we could view the entire room. Its gilded wooden chairs and beige upholstery, its white tablecloths and pink roses in crystal vases seemed more like a stage set than a restaurant.

"We did it!" exclaimed Liselotte. For an hour or so we were part of the grown-up world of Berlin. We ordered hot chocolate and cream puffs, watched the animated crowd, and talked about our families. Liselotte's older sister had been married the previous year and now had a baby.

"Do you know about babies and that sort of thing?" my friend quizzed me.

In this adult setting permeated with romance and intrigue, I camouflaged my ignorance and nodded knowingly.

Across the tables, through the haze of smoke and half hidden by numerous waitresses scurrying back and forth, a familiar face drifted into view. Of all people, I detected the Baroness in deep conversation with an imposing and well-dressed middle-aged man.

Surrounded by love,
Guided by hope.
Thus, walk through life accompanied by luck.

From your Anita
March 22, 1935

"What are you staring at?" wondered Liselotte, as she followed my glance.

"It's the Baroness!" Painstakingly I described my fascination with this idol. Our eyes followed the couple's gestures and movements avidly. We gaped at their lips, hoping to decipher their conversation, an unlikely feat since a wide-brimmed red hat, matching her dress, hid the Baroness's face from view. All we could see were clusters of fat cherries attached to the ribbon on her hat which bounced to the rhythm of her emphatic head movements.

Her companion too seemed fascinated by her. His eyes did not for a moment leave the Baroness's as they discussed, what seemed from afar, serious matters. We watched intently as he helped her into her fur coat and gently guided her out of the restaurant.

Had she seen me? But even if she had, neither of us ever made reference to this occasion.

For the rest of the afternoon, Liselotte and I created scenarios of their possible relationship from that of brother and sister, to lovers or to spies involved in international intrigues. Whenever we met for walks or ski outings, we continued to embellish on this topic with vast imaginative leaps, but never ever learned the truth.

I must have fallen asleep, because suddenly I wake to my father's voice. Light is shining through the cracks of the door. I'm out of bed and in his arms. He is home, he is back with us. But his looks have changed. His usually cheerful and clear eyes look tired, sad. His skin is a bland gray, his shoulder stooped. In one day he has aged. What ghosts have accosted him?

"It's too late now to tell you about my day," he says. "It was the most frightening day of my life. If we don't leave, quickly, I too will be arrested like countless other men. Sunday morning we are off to Holland! The plane tickets are in my pocket."

JULIAN SCHYBILSKI
CIRCA 1916

CHAPTER 2
JULIAN FROM PLESCHEN

I think of my early childhood as life in a bubble, devoid of consciousness and awareness, as though existence in my mother's womb had continued long after birth. I followed a prescribed, tireless routine of eating, walking, sleeping and being a good and obedient child to my good Mutti and my good Vati.

That my parents were separate people, with a separate life, never occurred to me. An unwavering predictability existed all around me. I was oblivious to cause and effect. The sun would rise, fresh rolls would make their early morning appearance at the back door without fail, beds would be made, rooms cleaned and food put on the table as if by magic.

My parents' presence was equally predictable and magical. Even during their occasional absence, their presence prevailed like our furniture — heavy, solid, omnipotent. The paintings, the silver candleholders and embroidered tablecloths all echoed their image. Even the maids, first Anna and Dedda, and later, Else, Fräulein Herta and a second Anna, reflected my parents' wishes and commands.

An unquestionable harmony and compatibility marked their life together though the turbulence of passion seemed missing. They walked together, napped together on the couch in my mother's dressing room, went out in the evening to undisclosed destinations, and disappeared into their private domain at bedtime. My brother and I existed strictly on the periphery of their lives. When my father was home from his business travels, my parents were inseparable. Only my mother's occasional indignation at my father's never-failing generosity toward his brother and sisters would arouse their tempers and voices. Yet even that ceased once my mother realized that nothing could curb my father's munificence. After all, we were not suffering as a result.

Our family communicated in a private language that was understood solely by the four of us, such as *Ernachen* for my mother and *Julchen* for my father. My mother addressed my father as *Schnuppus*. At different times, he referred to my mother as *das gute Schnuppäckchen*. I was called, at different times, *das kleine Schnuppäckchen*, *Rieke* or *Motte*. I never bothered to inquire as to the meaning or origin of this in-language which acted like caresses from an earlier perfect life.

This in-language also comprised an entire body of sayings that in themselves had no significance, yet from repeated usage took on meaning. Three expressions in particular come to mind: *der Hahn hat genappt* (the cock has pecked), *die Kuh ist üeber's Dach geflogen* (the cow flew over the moon), and *Grossmutter ist die älteste,* (Grandmother is the oldest). The latter meant, "Grandma knows best, this is it;" the first two — "so what else is new?"

I believe my parents were happy, in an uncomplicated way. My mother's passivity and ineptness in all practical matters complemented my father's energy and his facility for anticipating, planning and organizing. My father would spearhead excursions, vacations, even parties. With ambivalence and uncertainty, usually up to the last moment of any decision, my mother would ultimately, though reluctantly, yield to his proposed schemes.

Essentially, my mother's hesitations attested to a discomfort with which she travelled outside of her accustomed surroundings. It never reflected a wish to rebel or negate my father's desires; she was merely awkward in social situations. There was little inventiveness or spontaneity in her conversations, and no facility for small talk. She was prone to express the obvious, and in making virtue of necessity, was overly critical and exclusive. Realizing that people with greater intellect or flair found her uninteresting, she withdrew into her shell. Only with her life-long girlfriend, Hilde Kamm, was she perfectly at ease.

While my father registered occasional irritation with some of my mother's peculiarities, he also chose to read into them a more finely tuned sensibility. In contrast to his own down-to-earth upbringing, in the small town of Pleschen, these qualities infused his existence and sense of self with a deeply desired aura of status and class.

"Ernachen is the finest and the best in the world," he

would proclaim to anyone present, at moments when the realization of his good fortune to have married this reserved woman of aristocratic bearing struck him anew. On such occasions, he would stroke my mother's cheek, not so much like a lover, but like a benign uncle stroking the cheek of his favorite niece.

My father's greater ease in expressing his feelings, genuine or otherwise, would be met by my mother with a mixture of appreciation and weariness. My mother's face would show amusement, diffidence or occasional contempt at my father's public expression of affection. She knew my father was not always faithful. Yet she loved him and ignored his transient liaisons. She may even have welcomed them, since the sexual aspect of their marriage did not hold great importance for her.

Yet, from the moment she met my father, my mother knew that she had met the man she would marry. His presence exuded joy and created a sense of well-being. Friends and acquaintances described him as *Kein Freund von Traurigkeit*, no friend of sorrow. He loved a good time and became the life of a party, pulling everyone along. He enjoyed a glass of wine, a shot of cognac, yet never in excess. By contrast, my mother regarded any sort of alcohol repugnant and never tasted more than a sip of champagne or wine, and then only at rare moments.

My father's frequent business trips, which kept him away for weeks at a time, created a void which my mother would fill with excessive sleeping, and taking to bed with intestinal complaints. When well, she went on buying sprees. Those purchases of blouses, hats, or dresses were more often than not returned to the stores the following day.

During my father's absences, the jokes at meals were missing, and the menu lacked luster. Not that our kitchen ever produced notable meals. The German bourgeoise cuisine was heavy on soups, overcooked roasts swimming in thick sauces, mushy potatoes and vegetables. Applesauce was a daily fare that made me shudder. Equally offensive was the weekly pièce de résistance: apple rice. It was a favorite with the rest of the family, especially with my brother, who on such occasions turned into a good eater. For me, however, not even browned butter and cinnamon sugar could rescue this dish from unpalatability.

Once my father was back home, all was well and safe with the world. He was the Pied Piper whose wit, charm and good looks attracted all who encountered him. My male cousins adored him and tried to emulate him; my girl cousins had a crush on him.

Yet underneath this exuberance and undeniable charisma

JULIAN IN HIS
EARLY 20s

lingered a sentimental and romantic soul. Listening with him to records he had purchased for our old, hand-cranked phonograph, I would see tears flow unabashedly to the sounds of Beethoven's Ninth or the works of Schubert. His favorite operas were *The Magic Flute* and *Rosenkavalier.* When his spirits were high, we heard him whistle tunes from them or from *The Merry Widow* or *Fledermaus.* Our Sunday walks through the Grunewald or hikes during summer vacations high in the Alps became joyful excursions punctuated by the sound of his whistling.

Then there was the family whistle. The trill of a five-tone sequence, with a slightly greater emphasis on the fourth note, announced from half a block away my father's return from the office for the noon meal. My ears welcomed him before my eyes could see him.

"Else, Mutti, Tante Toni!" I would cry out, "Vati is coming! We can eat!"

My father's gait had a bounce to it, and as he strode along the street, his fingers lightly brushed the walls of the apartment buildings, as if his love of life overflowed even from his fingertips. In his presence, the rooms with the bombastic furniture looked cheerful, the monotonous, unimaginative meals were edible, the maids perked up and Tante Toni became full of smiles. My mother's stomach problems subsided and she appeared at lunch and dinner.

Never having gone beyond a basic education in his native Pleschen, my father was virtually self-taught. He was an avid reader, and kept Goethe's *Conversation with Eckermann*, a small, dark-brown leather book with gold lettering, next to his bed. He quoted from it often and reminded us, and possibly himself, that the book was a present from his closest childhood friend, Werner Meinicke, who, much to my father's continuous sorrow, was killed in the Great War. His animated intellect, his love of theater and music, had rubbed off on my father. I remember seeing my father sitting in bed, his head propped on two large pillows, holding the book close to his eyes, concentrating on every line. At other times, I would find him hunched over the book as he sat in one of our wicker armchairs on the small terrace that adjoined my parents' bedroom.

Tucked away in the corner of that terrace stood a cabinet which, in winter, stored kilos of unsalted butter my father had brought back from his business travels in Denmark. In late spring, dark red geraniums in green flower baskets along the ledge of the terrace surrounded and hid him, giving him the illusion of being far from the center of Berlin. Yet the street sounds of the city filtered through the air: the hissing of streetcars as their wheels made contact with the suspended electrical lines; the hum of occasional cars or delivery trucks; the chant of *Blumenerde* [potting soil] pelted out by the squat little man in black who guided his horse-drawn cart with the potting soil through the streets of our district of *Wilmersdorf*. The sounds signaled Spring, trips to the outskirts of Berlin to view the cherry blossoms, summer dresses, ankle socks and hopscotch in the Preussen Park.

JULIAN READING ON THE TERRACE, CIRCA 1936. POTTED GERANIUMS APPEAR THROUGH THE WINDOW SILL.

Little did I realize at the time the profound impact my father's reading of Goethe had on my as yet unformed mind. Not only would my father's enthusiasm evoke the taste of Danish butter, the bitter rancid smell of freshly planted geraniums or the memory of delicate cherry blossoms quivering in the spring breeze, but Goethe also became a family bible and foundation for my Weltanschauung.

Quotations would fill the family realm and were dropped with relish. "To have knowledge is salutary" might seem surprising in view of our otherwise less than intellectual milieu. Yet it did suggest the complexity of my father's personality.

"We retain from our learning, finally, only that part that we are able to use in a practical manner," he would quote. My father valued order, clear thinking; he abhorred clutter and waste to the point of saving the waxed paper in which his mid-morning sandwiches were wrapped. "Our life is short. We must try to find pleasure in one another," he underlined in his little book. "To love and be loved and not to miss out on the pleasure of the moment" was a *leitmotif* in his life and seemed fundamental to his existence.

It had been my father's good luck to be born to parents who had made peace with the insecurities, anxieties and losses of their earlier lives and who looked hopefully toward the future. The year of my father's birth, 1885, found my Grandfather Isaac economically secure and much in love with Johanna, his second wife, a beautiful, strong and intelligent woman who brought order and serenity into his previously chaotic life.

Isaac Schybilski, a person of volatile passions, had lost his first wife, leaving in his care four unruly children: two sons, Salo and Benno, and two daughters, Rosa and Toni, ranging in ages from eight to fourteen. Johanna won the love of her stepchildren, and presented Isaac with two more sons: first Martin, a rather sickly child, and then Julian, my father, a happy and healthy cherub.

While never an exceptional student, he was smart enough, and gifted with sound common sense. He was one of the boys. The teachers favored him, ignored his pranks and predicted a successful future.

I loved to listen to my father tell about his Pleschen

Julian, age 6, the teacher's favorite.

childhood, with its easy and jovial life that evoked in me an enchantment and delight. Even the rich sound of the word Pleschen charmed me. My father told about walking barefoot along cobblestone or dirt roads with chickens fluttering at his heels. Cows grazed on adjacent farms, and everyone knew everyone else.

It was in Pleschen that he made his initial forays into the world of business. Once school was out for the day, he ran errands, swept floors or wrapped packages in his father's general store. The store was located in the center of the village, facing the market square. Nearby were the local bank and a small stationery shop, both owned by the parents of Martin's future wife, Rosel. On market days, Polish farmers, rich German landowners and local folk met in the village square to catch up on the latest happenings amidst the chatter of the vendors who proudly displayed their produce. On those days, my grandfather's store hummed with the chatter of customers in search of a dress, a suit, meters of fabric or a needle. My father thrived on this pandemonium and lived from one school vacation to the next, to spend entire days in the store, where, with ears and eyes wide open, he learned about people, business, and life in general.

My father's vivid recollections of Pleschen market days, of the horse-drawn carts stopping at Schybilski and Sons, of his scrubbing and sweeping, and of moonlit village dances to the sound of gypsy music, kept me a spellbound and insatiable listener. Indeed, it was only in the imagination that Pleschen existed for me. By the time I was born, my grandparents were long dead and Onkel Martin, who for a while had carried on the family business, had in 1920 followed my father to Berlin. The national fate of Pleschen, situated in the Polish Corridor, always depended on the victor of the most recent war. After World War I, Pleschen became Polish again. Its German residents were given the choice to remain or to leave, and my uncle chose the latter.

Johanna and Isaac were devout Jews for whom being Jewish was a way of life. Without being excessively dogmatic, they observed all customs and rituals. They could joke at the rabbi's dull sermons or poke fun at fellow Jews and the Jewish predicament without fearing retribution from an angry or vengeful God. But they also knew that, as a long-persecuted minority, self-reliance and astuteness were essential to survival, and they hoped to instill these traits in their children.

The Jewish population of Pleschen was no longer confined within a ghetto, and my father never mentioned offensive remarks concerning his Jewishness. While all the Schybilski children attended Hebrew school, and circumcision and Bar Mitzvah were taken for granted, they also went to the local public school. In the 1890s, this pointed to an early move toward westernization and emancipation. My grandparents considered themselves patriotic Germans and were not drawn to the cause of Zionism that Theodore Herzl began to popularize. Thus, my father grew up in easy-going, tolerant and conservative surroundings with parents whose confidence in him proved to be well justified.

The prediction of my father's teachers were equally validated. He became the star of the family. Salo, his older half-brother, left Pleschen in late adolescence and settled in Berlin. A drifter, he died of syphilis at an early age. The twelve-year-old Benno was shipped off to America in the early 1890s because my grandfather considered him a hopeless failure. Throughout my Berlin childhood, Onkel Benno appeared at regular intervals, bearing a cornucopia of gifts. None of us, however, found much use for the porcelain ballerinas, the scarves in bold colors, and the gaudy jewelry. Even the baseball mitt was unsuccessful since my brother had neither the opportunity nor the skill to deal with this uniquely American artifact.

Onkel Benno was a fine looking man, slimly built with

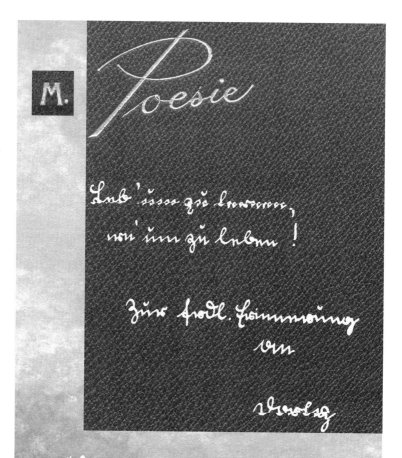

LIVE TO LEARN,
LEARN TO LIVE.

IN FRIENDLY REMEMBRANCE OF

DORLEY
NOVEMBER 10, 1935

delicate features, a docile smile. His expensive suits, monogrammed shirts with constantly changing neckties, and beautiful shoes said clearly, "I've made it in this world." Yet we all remained mystified about how our American uncle earned a living. Nebulous answers to occasional queries became lost in his cigar smoke.

Our jolly bachelor uncle's good grooming lost some of its appeal, however, by his continuous gum-chewing, which we viewed as a typically American uncivilized habit. "Only cows chew, namely grass," muttered my father, eyes and eyebrows raised.

My mother showed similar exasperation when at dinner Onkel Benno would say 'I am full' when offered another helping. "How vulgar," she groaned in loathing. "Why can't he say, 'No, thank you.'?"

Another one of his quirks was his continuous jingling of money in his pants' pocket. I remember my mother's pained expression. Money for her was a necessary evil, but one never to be displayed. "Someone should tell him to stop that," she hissed as she left the room in disgust.

Dressed in his beautiful suits and occasionally sporting spats, Onkel Benno used to sit for hours in one of the overstuffed leather easy chairs in the living room. Smoking and sucking the soaked tips of cigars, scattering ash all around him, my mother endured him in silent fury.

Yet I always liked my bachelor uncle. He was a quiet, good-natured man who floated in and out of our lives inaudibly, unobtrusively, with no apparent need or wish for sustained attachment. He remained a strange and unfamiliar figure, with his few American expressions like *swell, dandy,* and *OK.*

I recognized the same serene and gentle quality in my Onkel Martin. His decision to remain in Pleschen to conduct the family business was more a matter of necessity and obligation than personal choice. He would have preferred to write poetry all day or sit in the local café, discussing ideas. But at twenty-five, Martin had married Rosel, his childhood sweetheart, and soon thereafter had become the father of Hanna and Steffi. He had to support a family. The combination of expediency and filial duty kept him in Pleschen, at least until after the war.

No one ever expected my father to remain in Pleschen. My grandfather was intent on seeing his favorite son succeed in the bigger world. A friend of his in Breslau (a three-hour train ride from Pleschen) had offered my father an

JOHANNA AND ISAAC
SCHYBILSKI

apprenticeship in his clothing business. The sixteen-year-old Julian, in a spiffy brand-new suit, was conducted by the entire family to the Pleschen train station for that first parting. A few bank notes, gifts for Johanna's cousins with whom he would live, and admonitions to be industrious, alert, obliging and helpful accompanied him as the conductor's whistle set the train in motion.

I never asked my father how he felt about leaving home. Suffice it to say that over the years, his ease with people, his charm mixed with intelligence, imagination and common sense made him a highly desirable employee. Effortlessly he climbed the ladder from apprentice to stock clerk to salesman and, eventually, owner of his own business.

World War I interrupted his business career. A photo of my father as a Prussian cavalryman shows a proud man, chest out, shoulders back, sitting securely in the saddle. The narrow visor on his cap hides his eyes but accentuates a small moustache that resembles a mouse. He avoids a photo smile. Lips pulled lengthwise, chin up, earnest, he appears like a benevolent aristocrat, at ease and in control. In a tight and trim uniform, he sits on his horse, Jo, whose shiny pelt illuminates the otherwise flat surface of the slightly discolored photo.

"Jo was prince," he said of his chestnut stallion. "The most intuitive and best fed horse. Nothing but grains and plants. His pelt shone like a diamond. He refused anyone to ride him, so I volunteered to train him. He first played hard-to-get, but finally gave in."

My father fought on the eastern front and was decorated with the Iron Cross second class for bravery in action. It gleamed briefly on his uniform, but eventually was relegated to the wicker basket from which we, as children, regularly pulled items to be used for our occasional theatrical performances.

With the end of the war and the death of Johanna and

JULIAN AS A PRUSSIAN CAVALRYMAN — A PROUD MAN, CHEST OUT, SHOULDERS BACK, SITTING SECURELY IN THE SADDLE.

Isaac, all members of the Schybilski family had left Pleschen. My father settled in Berlin, where, much to the disappointment of his Breslau employer-friend, he joined the clothing firm of Bruck and Löwenstein. He lived the life of a merry and greatly pursued bachelor, until he met my mother in 1921.

In addition to Onkel Martin and his family, Tante Toni who by then had married an old family friend, Kurt Wolf, moved to Berlin as well. Tante Rosa, my father's other half-sister, married a school teacher and settled in Stettin, a small town on the Baltic Sea.

Succeeding in the big city proved to be more complex and perilous than anyone had expected. Only the strong would survive. My father did and became the focal point and support of his family.

ERNA LÖWENBERG
CIRCA 1910

CHAPTER 3
ERNA FROM GÖRLITZ

Marrying Erna Löwenberg from Görlitz gave my father the springboard to a new life, one of predictable comfort, reliability and restraint, qualities not particularly stressed in Pleschen. His straightforward and unpretentious family

had never attempted to be anything they were not. They never doubted their own dignity nor their place in the world. They were emotional. Feelings of anger, joy or disappointment were openly displayed not only within the family, but among neighbors and acquaintances as well.

Both my grandfathers were known for their choleric tempers. However, the Schybilskis openly acknowledged those eruptions, accepting them, fighting back or ridiculing them. Johanna never loved her husband any less for his outbursts.

Alexander Löwenberg's explosions, by contrast, closed doors and curtains. My gentle and intimidated grandmother Lina hauled the children to their rooms. There they hovered,

ALEXANDER
LÖWENBERG
CIRCA 1885

Lina
Löwenberg
Circa 1890

cowed and fearful, hoping the maids would not witness this embarrassment, or worse yet, tell the neighbors. Lina never responded in kind; her primary task was the protection of her children Erna, Valli and Herman.

Undoubtedly, the Schybilski clan never felt entirely comfortable with the Löwenberg family's more restrained manners and air of superiority. But they respected them, and for the sake of Julian and his happiness, kept their reservations to themselves.

My mother came from a long line of family that had lived and married in Silesia. Over the decades, they maintained close and affectionate ties with a network of relatives whose interests included farming, canning, distilling and banking. My grandfather Löwenberg's astute judgment on all matters concerning the Jewish and non-Jewish communities were highly regarded, and he was consulted for advice by many.

In the Löwenberg household, the ordinary was never considered quite good enough. The "right" clothes and jewelry could be found only in the finest stores in Berlin, a four-hour train ride from Görlitz. Furniture was made to order, linens specially embroidered and the circle of friends carefully chosen for their refinement and good taste.

The circumscribed expectations and the tensions surrounding my grandfather's unpredictable behavior did leave their mark on my mother. She was unsure of herself, fearful and reserved in new situations, and excessively concerned with manners, behavior and bodily functions. Her inhibitions allowed little exuberance and laughter. Only later in life did she become more comfortable with herself and her feelings.

"If I could do it all over again," she said many years later, "I would have loved to study medicine. For my father, that would have been out of the question."

My mother spent her young adult life in Victorian style in her parents' house, as an obedient and helpful daughter. She embroidered napkins and handkerchiefs, read French books and took endless walks with her friend, Hilde Kamm, and their dogs, Spitz and Fips.

All the snapshots in the photograph albums attested to the fact that my mother was a beautiful young woman — tall and svelt with slender hips and shapely breasts. Her sister, Valli, who had married Julius Broh, a well-to-do merchant in Danzig, and my mother portrayed two dazzling young women in long, elegant embroidered dresses and wide-brimmed hats. Their long gloves hid fingernails undoubtedly manicured with the polisher from the ivory-handled manicure set.

ERNA
CIRCA 1910

VALLI AND
ERNA
CIRCA 1917

Valli and Erna, five years apart, were an inseparable pair. After Valli's marriage in 1912, Danzig was my mother's second home where she became a "second mother" to her nephews, Erich and Fritz. Perhaps her most prized memories were of those summers. Escorted by young naval officers in white uniforms, who were temporarily stationed by the waters of the Baltic, the two sisters would leisurely promenade along the boardwalk. Their destination was the bandstand where, sheltered under parasols, they applauded the navy band's playing of marches and waltzes, and where they watched vendors sell candied walnuts and lemonade to a happy crowd.

During the summer months before the onset of World War I, Danzig served as the summer residence for the German crown prince and princess, who, with their retinue, were often sighted among the visitors. My mother recounted with delight the occasion when the crown princess presented her with a silver candy bowl. Had my mother won it in a raffle? I cannot remember. Two joined hands on its base were embossed with the inscription *Manus Manum Lavat* (one hand washes the other). Supported atop a base of inch-high slender silver feet, the bowl seemed to float.

I loved the bowl's oval shape and occasionally helped our maids, Else or Anna, polish it. In shiny splendor, it was then restored to its place on the dining-room buffet, filled with my mother's favorite ginger sticks or chocolate covered coffee beans. The significance of the inscription did not escape my notice, and over the years became included in the many family phrases that led to a generous and tender world view.

This silver bowl evoked long-gone qualities of an era where genuine value was placed on discretion, gentility and beauty, and where the idea of leisure was developed to perfection. A staff of servants attended to Valli's every need. They were hired so that their mistress would not have to be involved in routine household duties. She spent her days paying visits to friends, to the seamstress for fittings, and taking leisurely strolls along the ocean front, accompanied by her two little boys and their governess.

Julius Broh adored his wife and considered her a jewel, unfailingly returning home for noon and evening meals so as to be near her. It gave him unmitigated pleasure to indulge all her whims and wishes, regardless of expense or effort. From her, he asked nothing but her presence.

Very little clouded the stable, uneventful routines of the

OH BELIEVE ME, WHEN IN CHILDHOOD,
A WARM MOTHER'S HEART IS BEATING.
NO MATTER WHO LOVES YOU, OH BELIEVE ME,
NO ONE EVER WILL CARE FOR YOU AS MUCH.
TO MY MARIANNE,

IN REMEMBRANCE OF

HELGA
BERLIN, SEPTEMBER 30, 1934

Löwenbergs and the Brohs. Even during the war, life at *Bautzener Strasse*, in Görlitz, continued with unaltered regularity. My mother and grandmother served as nurse's aides at the local army hospitals. My grandfather's business prospered, as he supplied the troops with spirits, wine and beer. No one in the family was affected by the food shortages and rationing. Meat, dairy products, fruit and vegetables kept appearing from longtime friends on neighboring farms, who had benefited from my Grandfather's generosity over the years. And Onkel Herman, an officer in the Provisions Corps, made equally sure that nothing was lacking at home.

It was not the battlefield, but the flu epidemic of 1918, that brought to a halt the confident and contented routine of my mother's life. Both she and Valli fell victims to its raging assault. My grandmother had hastened to Danzig to help nurse her two daughters whose high fever and delirium lasted for days. And it was she who had to break the tragic news to my slowly recovering mother that Valli had died. I don't believe that my mother ever totally recovered from this devastating loss.

For the rest of her life, dreams of Valli disturbed her sleep. In the delirium of a later serious illness, she accused my father of not having told her that Valli had died.

A strong bond developed between my mother and her two nephews. She became an ally in their struggles with the intractable Julius and a confidante for life. Valli's memory was further kept alive by my mother's frequent stories of their girlhood together, by the many photographs displayed throughout our apartment and by my carrying "Valli" as my middle name. My aunt's premature death created in my mother a terror of even the mildest illness. She always imagined the worst.

With the end of the war and the process of coming to terms with Valli's death, life returned to its accustomed routine. My mother was approaching thirty and while her family began to worry that she would remain an old maid, my mother apparently had many opportunities to marry. Yet none of the suitors were "right." They seemed too materialistic, too short, too heavy, humorless or dull. The thought of waking up next to any one of those men was unthinkable. She would rather remain single. After all, her life was not disagreeable.

Family solidarity and a genuine wish to promote the well-being of those closest were features common to the Schybilskis and the Löwenbergs. Thus it had not been inappropriate for my Onkel Martin to travel to Görlitz late in 1919 to establish connections between the two families. Mutual friends had suggested that Erna and Julian, two eligible and attractive individuals, should meet. Alexander Löwenberg considered such family introductions quite in order. He acknowledged the difficulty young Jewish women had in meeting suitable marriage partners. And no doubt it did not escape Martin's awareness that his younger brother's sowing of wild oats should come to an end.

Julian's 135-mile train trip to Görlitz followed soon after Martin's warmly received inspection foray. The ground work had been laid for a successful outcome. Erna and Julian liked each other immediately. Perhaps they even fell in love.

My mother knew she had found the perfect companion, though she could never say exactly why he was so "right." No doubt his vibrancy and charm endowed her with attributes she felt she lacked. My father was enchanted with the beauty and reticence of the woman who was to become his bride. Both families supported the union, and delighted in the forthcoming marriage.

Furthermore, every indication pointed to a successful business career for my father. At the time of meeting my mother, my father was employed as general manager for Bruck and Löwenstein, a Berlin men's clothing factory with wholesale and retail outlets throughout Germany. But

THE WEDDING
OF JULIAN AND
ERNA SCHYBILSKI
DECEMBER 26, 1921

Julian's thoughts already anticipated a time when he would start a business on his own.

My father's weekend courting trips from Berlin to Görlitz were supplemented by ardent letters whose poetry and sensitivity touched my mother and confirmed to her that this was the man for her. Brotherly discretion prevented my mother from ever learning that the splendid letters issued from the pen of Martin, whose eloquence far surpassed my father's undistinguished style.

The marriage license was signed in Görlitz on December 26, 1921. My mother, who usually wrote in a stiff hand, documented her new status by writing in bold, loose letters the name which was now, for better or worse, hers: "Erna Schybilski." She knew that she had drawn the trump card.

My father felt likewise. At age 36, he was more than ready to bid farewell to life as the carefree bachelor. He was warmly welcomed into an established family and was marrying "the best and finest in the world."

The wedding celebration took place at the Hotel Vier Jahreszeiten (Four Seasons) in Dresden. From Berlin, Stettin, Danzig, and Görlitz, seventeen of the closest relatives travelled to the event. Only Tante Valli was missing.

The bridegroom arrived with top hat, in an elegant morning coat, and gleaming white shirt and bow tie. Trailing behind was a contented Erna in a simple white chiffon ankle-length dress and a white cap around which a soft white veil fluttered. Her gloved hand held a bouquet of white roses and primroses.

Throughout my childhood, I heard accounts of the eight-course dinner, the wine and champagne that flowed freely, the toasts, songs and poems especially composed for the occasion and the music by Strauss and Offenbach that accompanied the feast. Beguiled, I used to inspect the hand-crafted leather box that contained all the wedding mementos and the gold-edged menu.

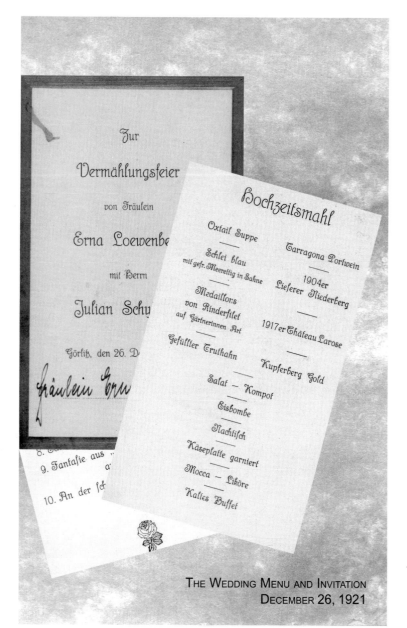

Zur

Vermählungsfeier

von Fräulein

Erna Loewenbe

mit Herrn

Julian Schu

Görlitz, den 26. D

8.

9. Fantasie aus

10. An der sch

Hochzeitsmahl

Oxtail Suppe

Schlei blau
mit gefr. Meerettig in Sahne

Medaillons
von Rinderfilet
auf Gärtnerinnen Art

Gefüllter Truthahn

Salat — Kompot

Eisbombe

Nachtisch

Käseplatte garniert

Mocca — Liköre

Kaltes Buffet

Tarragona Portwein

1904er
Lieserer Niederberg

1917er Château Larose

Kupferberg Gold

THE WEDDING MENU AND INVITATION
DECEMBER 26, 1921

Oxtail Soup
Porto from Tarragon

Supreme of Filet of Sole
1904 Lieser Niederberg

Medallions of Filet of Beef
with Garden Vegetables
1917 Chateau la Rose

Gelatine of Capon
Kupferberg Gold

Salad - Cheese

Bombe Glacée - Macedone of Fruit - Pastries

Mocca
Liqueurs

Cold Buffet

THE WEDDING MENU TRANSLATED

A dowry of sliver, dishes, crystal, bedding and towels duly monogrammed "ELS" accompanied the newlyweds to Berlin. Their first apartment was on Tielewardenberger Strasse, close to the Rivers Havel and Spree and ten minutes by foot from the Tiergarten. Awaiting them was Anna, the Löwenbergs' young maid, who was now to care for the young couple and for me, once I arrived on the scene.

Although I never knew Pleschen or my Pleschen grandparents, I can vividly remember Görlitz and my Görlitz grandparents. Their large living quarters were conveniently located above my grandfather's brewery, *Wilhelm Ziemer*. In the small adjacent *Kneipe* (bar) on the *Bautzener Strasse*, the locals congregated for their daily schnapps. It was a well-run establishment, where bad behavior and drunks were not tolerated. The regulars dropped in throughout the day, but at night it was closed. Men of all sizes and ages, always with hat or cap, were perched on bar stools, their mugs or glasses on the solid, well-used oak bar. They made a big fuss over me, Herr Löwenberg's little granddaughter from Berlin, during the frequent visits with my mother. Some had already fussed over her when she was a girl.

To the right of the *Kneipe*, an arched doorway opened onto a courtyard whose large gray cobblestones made walking difficult. The stones did not trouble the horses or interfere with the carriages or the barrels of beer and wine stored in neatly partitioned spaces at the edge of the courtyard.

Having lived all her early life near those weathered vats and barrels, my mother seemed impervious to their rich and pungent smells. Yet all through my life, the smells of breweries, wine cellars and taverns instantaneously evoke a familiar and distant Görlitz. These memories included not only the tantalizing odors of fermentation, but also the feeling of safety and comfort of being held on the laps of my grandmother or Frau Lange, my grandparents' faithful maid and general factotum. Her husband was the head coachman, who, right out of school in 1880, was hired by my great-grandfather.

Nestled on someone's lap, as a two-year-old, I watched from the upstairs window as horses were harnessed and connected to barrel-laden carts only to disappear to unknown destinations. On all fours, I learned to make my way up and down the beautiful, but poorly lit, circular staircase that led to my grandparents' living quarters. There, warmth and serenity filled the tastefully furnished rooms, whose only connecting link with the world downstairs was that all-pervasive smell of beer and wine, in heavy barrels that seemed to have been anchored in their places forever.

Before my father entered my mother's life, her brother Herman was her faithful friend and companion. Their special closeness continued even after they were both married. As a matter of fact, it was my mother who introduced Herman to his future wife. Else Gradnauer, a fair-haired, graceful young woman from a "good" German-Jewish family, hailed from Berlinchen, a town slightly northeast of Berlin. In a smocked white dress, I served as flower girl at their wedding in 1925.

Younger by ten years than my mother, Tante Else had benefited from a more enlightened attitude towards the education of women. She had attended secretarial school, and on her frequent visits to Berlin, impressed me with her splendid typing and miraculous shorthand skills. Like learning the Morse Code, I considered these unattainable achievements and admired her mastery and independence. We used to receive her typewritten letters, which my father greeted with joyful relief. He could never decipher the handwritten ones.

After Alexander's death, Onkel Herman took control of the brewery. The Görlitz-Berlin family ties remained fully intact and visits back and forth were regular and happy events. The world seemed young and new, and the future looked bright, provided that hard work was infused with a sprinkling of goodwill, luck and some financial backing.

JEANETTE RAPHAELSOHN, LINA'S MOTHER AND MARIANNE'S GREAT-GRANDMOTHER, IN ALLENSTEIN, EAST PRUSSIA, SHELLING PEAS CIRCA 1900

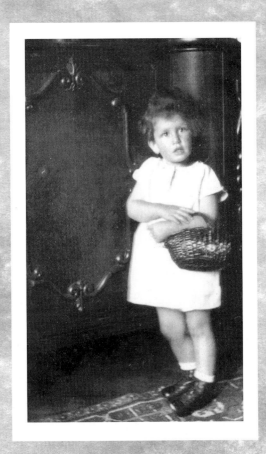

MARIANNE
1927

One ring was for Else, the housekeeper and cook, two for Fräulein Herta, the governess, three for me and four for Tante Toni. We were thus summoned to appear in whatever part of our apartment my mother happened to be. Mostly, we would be called

MARIANNE 1924

to her bedroom or dressing room to receive orders and comments, or merely to be asked to keep her company. At other times, the rings would emanate from the dining room table. There my mother pressed the small button on a beautiful flat round silver disk with inlaid purple stones. It was attached to a chord, which was threaded through a hole in the carpet and fastened to a mysterious subterranean outlet. One ring indicated that we were ready to be served, two meant that the dishes could be removed.

A rectangular wooden box, fastened to the wall in a small alcove, outside the kitchen and immediately above the wall telephone indicated the source of the rings. A small numbered flap dropped to signify the ring's provenance and, having been noted, was dutifully replaced by Else to its original position.

The young and ostensibly naive Erna from Görlitz ruled her household by merely putting her fingertips to a bell, often from her bed. Else would be instructed about the menu for the day, the shopping, the chores. Fräulein Herta was

MARIANNE 1927

told what my little brother and I were to wear and reminded of our various after-school activities. Tante Toni was beckoned to chat, provided my mother was in an expansive mood. However, more often than not, she preferred to be left alone, under her green satin quilted bed covers whose small pearl buttons kept the embroidered linen sheets from Görlitz securely fastened.

Imagining the way my classmates' mothers spent their days by actively caring for their families, I was embarrassed by the futility surrounding my mother's daily routine. Family loyalty, however, precluded my ever admitting to that publicly. She was never up and about when I left for school. She spent her days on shopping trips, or on outings to the market, to her dressmaker, to the hairdresser, or to Frau Sänger, *die Schönheitskönigin* (the beauty queen) for her weekly facial.

After her outings, my mother came home in time to have lunch, to nap, to supervise my homework or to simply sit by my side during my afternoon piano practice sessions.

My mother did not share my father's passion for books and ideas. Occasionally, and with gusto, she launched on knitting projects which were, however, seldom completed.

MARIANNE, ERNA,
HANS AND JULIAN,
SUMMER OF 1929
IGLS, AUSTRIA

She was sick a lot. Chronic migraines, intestinal ailments, and respiratory infections kept her in bed for days at a time. Her curtains were tightly shut, the telephone was unplugged, and my brother and I had to tiptoe through the halls, opening and closing doors with care.

Her bouts with intestinal upsets lasted the longest. Dr. Grünbaum, a lascivious and to my childlike mind macabre person, appeared with his mysterious, pouchy black leather bag. He routinely administered some form of medicinal potion, and insisted on bed rest, an order my mother seemed to accept with pleasure. He put my mother on a diet of thin oatmeal soup, cooked in nothing but water. I can still see her, propped on her pillow, her hair tousled around her ears, guiding the large silver spoon full of horrible gruel to her mouth, and swallowing it with relish.

Dr. Grünbaum sometimes let me hold his bag as he put on his overcoat. With his freed hand he seized the opportunity to slyly stroke my face or shoulders, muttering "My, what a pretty girl you are," as I hastily escaped.

Although my mother's presence was ubiquitous, her aloofness created a void that made me turn to other members of the household. A creeping emptiness used to gnaw in my stomach during those endless days of her unavailability, when schoolwork was done and there were no friends to visit. Surreptitiously, I would sneak into the kitchen, our maid Else's domain. More often than not, I would be caught looking without finding. To eat between meals was strictly forbidden. A possible exception was the occasional purchase of a dry roll during the thirty-minute walk home with Fräulein Herta from weekly gymnastic lessons. No doubt my mother felt that Major Böhmer's rigorous exercises merited a token of indulgence. The far more desirable cinnamon snails or jam-filled doughnuts, the famous *Berliner Pfannkuchen*, were emphatically forbidden.

On those empty days, when I felt annoyed at having to

MARIANNE AND HER FAMILY OF
DOLLS IN A WICKER CARRIAGE
1929

tiptoe through the halls of the apartment, I needed to seek out someone for companionship. Fräulein Herta was occupied with my little brother. Tante Toni might be on her weekly expedition to the lending library and the living and dining rooms were off limits.

At such times, Else's room, past the hall with the wall telephone and through the kitchen, became my refuge. Away from the center of our family life, her quarters drew me like a magnet. Located by the back door, Else was free to receive any visitor she chose without any of us knowing. According to Frau Zeck, numerous gentleman callers would make their way up the dark circular stairway and quietly knock on her door. They were cheerfully received.

Else welcomed me with delight as well when I came knocking at her door. It opened to minuscule quarters, where a wardrobe and chest of drawers left barely enough room for the bed. Invariably I would sink down on the puffy, unruly comforter that hid the rumpled bedclothes. Sitting or lying next to one another, we consumed contraband items such as chocolates, candies or cakes — allies in treason. By the head of the bed towered a radio in the shape of an oval bird cage; it transmitted enticing sounds of the current tangos and foxtrots, to which Else seemed to know all the lyrics.

In that small room, filled with her special smell — a mixture of sweet perfume and cheap soap that drifted off her fleshy skin — Else entertained me for hours on end with horror stories of her growing up in a one-room cottage near Königsberg, in eastern Prussia on the Bay of Danzig where her father repaired shoes in an adjoining shed. There was never enough food to go around and her mother did cleaning and washing for an aristocratic family in town. Else, the youngest child, went along, and played with the children who owned toys whose existence she never had imagined, beautiful clothes, and who were never hungry. Periodically, Frau von Ebingen passed her children's outgrown clothes on to Else. During hunting season, Else spent the nights there, while her mother, with a huge staff of cooks, maids and butlers, worked behind the scenes to ensure the success of a house party. Else told me about the important people who used to arrive, some in horse-drawn carriages, others in convertible motor cars, with passengers draped in heavy fur blankets and tight-fitting leather caps with earflaps. Even Field Marshall von Hindenburg once made a brief appearance.

Else had been with our family since 1930, when we moved to the larger, more elegant apartment on Brandenburgischen Strasse. By that time, my parents had outgrown their first Berlin apartment on Tielewardenberg Strasse. My father's aspiration to start his own business had become a reality in 1925. He and Alfred Silberstein, an associate from Bruck and Löwenstein, went into partnership, and established the men's clothing firm of Silberstein and

Schybilski, near Alexanderplatz, Poststrasse 7-8.

At the time of the move, our devoted caretaker, Anna, returned to Görlitz and married a recently widowed neighboring farmer. During her eight years with our family, she had spoiled and cared for my mother as if she had been her own child. She was present at my birth and at that of my little brother. She cooked, sewed, ironed, attended the sick, and made noble efforts to get along with the nurses who were added at the arrival of a new baby. She comforted my mother when my grandmother died shortly before my brother's birth, and accompanied my parents to Görlitz for the funeral.

She had spoiled me as well. Once when my mother had

ANNA AND
MARIANNE
1924

MARIANNE
CIRCA 1926

punished me by depriving me of all sweets, Anna, notwithstanding her orders, had taken me to a café on her afternoon off and treated me to a cream puff. Confronted with this unpardonable sin, she replied, "But with me, Mariannchen was not naughty."

When Else first came to us in 1930, she was a hefty 19-year-old, an unpolished country girl. With astounding skill, my mother transformed her into an efficient and energetic servant who followed orders to perfection. Yet she never lost her simplicity and earthiness, the qualities that drew me so strongly to her. Being with her was like taking a warm bath. All was comfort and ease. She scratched my back, and just like kids, we would tickle one another underneath her fluffy comforter.

On Fräulein Herta's afternoons off, my brother and I

would run wildly around the living room table with Else, then hide in wait under its heavy oak top to peek up her skirts, which most of the time revealed a dark-haired nakedness and offered us a glimpse into a hidden world. Noticing our engrossed attention, she would move away, chuckling and protesting that we were impossible children.

While my mother, Fräulein Herta and Tante Toni maintained an inscrutable modesty, Else's occasional bare breasts, exposed when I unexpectedly appeared on her doorstep, partially satisfied my curiosity. This permitted me to intimate to my classmates that the various Venuses we viewed on trips to the *Staats* or *Pergamon Museums* were nothing compared with the real thing.

The pursuit of a live male body presented far greater

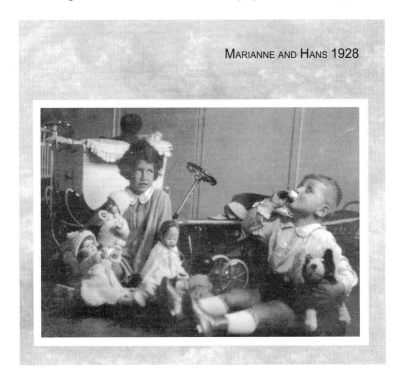

MARIANNE AND HANS 1928

complexities. Notwithstanding the occasional marble nude in museums, or some man's need to expose himself to a petrified ten-or-eleven-year-old on darkened street corners or behind the bushes of the Preussen Park, male nakedness was elusive. Yet childlike curiosity prevailed. One summer in particular, at the Danish beach resort of Skaagen, my Danish friend, Sigrid Kuntz, and I made an inordinate number of trips to the changing cabins of the bath houses. Impatiently we took turns, peeking through the holes of the wooden partitions, to spy on men in the process of changing in and out of their long-legged swimming suits. Much to our regret, our endeavors were often cut short by our parents' plans for excursions or by the arrival of mothers with their offspring, subjects of no interest to us.

Sigrid confided how she would spy through the keyhole of her room, which adjoined the bathroom, waiting for the arrival of her father, in the nude, for his morning bath. One morning, though, her father had moved the towel bar so that it now covered the peep-hole. What an embarrassment! Yet nothing was ever said about it. Our curiosity with these yet puzzling enigmas only strengthened our friendship. We remained devoted pen pals for many years, despite Hitlerian edicts forbidding communication between Jew and gentile.

With her stories, her presence, and her directness, Else in the kitchen contributed much to my growing awareness of the world. She opened my eyes and ears to a life less genteel and predictable than ours.

In front of me, my parents maintained an icy silence when discussing problems they deemed not for me to hear. Not so Else. One of her brothers, Kuno, had been in jail for stealing. On her days off, she visited him, loaded with bags of candy, cigarettes, and an occasional bottle of schnapps which may well have come out of the Schybilski grocery budget, elevating Kuno to a bona fide family member.

After his release from prison, my father found him a job

HANS, ERNA,
AND MARIANNE,
SUMMER ON
THE BALTIC 1930

in a cement factory as a janitor. He used to visit us during those years and, over a cup of coffee and a cigarette in the kitchen, would recount how he and his workers were being recruited for the SA, *Sturmabteiling* — the rank and file membership in the Nazi party. Those not joining were liable to lose their jobs. What should he do? He did not want to be out of work. My father was consulted when he came into the kitchen to shine his shoes or to enlist me to shine them for him.

"The SA are nothing but a bunch of hoodlums. They can't be taken seriously. Why not join?" said my father.

Kuno's swarthy looks appealed to me. Like Else, he was endowed with an insouciant cheerfulness. Always ready to crack a joke in his particular mixture of Berlinese and

Be like the sundial and count only the cheerful hours.

In remembrance

your Flora
Berlin, October 28, 1935

Pomeranian German, he gave the appearance of being devoid of all malice or seriousness, hardly a suitable recruit for the Nazi party.

Once in a while he was accompanied by a thin young girl whom he introduced as his girlfriend. At other times, he arrived with another sister, Fanny, who was pregnant but never brought a husband. Else found her a temporary job in a bakery. A pittance of a supplement from Else, and from my parents, saw her through the pregnancy. Once Fanny had given birth to a healthy baby girl, she did not place her for adoption, as planned. One of the young bakers had fallen in love with her and they married when the baby was three months old.

It wasn't on the school bench, but around our shiny white kitchen table, drinking café au lait with two cubes of sugar, eating almond-paste coffee cake or jam doughnuts, which Else had specially bought for her visitors, that I learned about love, sex, adoptions and the hazards of womanhood in a precarious world.

My life in that kitchen was acknowledged by my mother with considerable distaste. Yet even she realized that she could not control my every move, though her nature compelled her otherwise. It was also evident that she had a growing affection for Else, especially since she was in part a product of her own creation.

Once Kuno had joined the Nazi party, he continued to visit our kitchen, but his visits became increasingly rare. He described the training, the marches, and the persuasiveness of Hitler, all of which began to leave no doubt in Kuno's mind that Hitler's vision was the way toward a glorious future for Germany. Hadn't the Treaty of Versailles destroyed the Fatherland, and didn't Germany need new moral fiber?

One evening in 1936, shortly before Else was forced to leave, Kuno asked to speak with my father. He thanked him profusely for all he had done for him in the past. But today would be the last time that he could come to visit. Socializing with non-Aryans was punishable by loss of job or even being sent to a labor camp.

"I had no idea it would come to this," he said to my father. "Hitler is getting stronger by the day, and the SA are no longer hoodlums. They have power. There is talk of prohibiting girls like my sister to work in Jewish households. Hitler is serious about wanting Germany free of Jews."

Kuno had been promoted to a top post in the Nazi party. He tried to convince my father that he knew what he was talking about. "Things will get much worse for the Jews," he warned. "You and your family must leave. This is all I can tell you. Now I must go."

He hugged me quickly as he told me to be nice to my little brother. With a sigh, he looked around and then he bolted out the kitchen door. Else locked and chained it resolutely as if she hoped to shut out all present and future danger.

As Kuno had predicted, Else had to leave our household. The Nüremberg laws that circumscribed the relationship between the German state and its Jewish population had ordained that no Aryan woman of child-bearing age was permitted to be employed in a Jewish household. I was saddened by Else's subsequent departure later that year, but not devastated. It did not cause me sleepless nights or tears. Her rambunctious, freewheeling personality had brought a breath of fresh air into our otherwise staid household routine. For me, she had been a companion with whom, for a moment, I could be the unrestrained child. Yet there was no deep bond.

Else's feelings about leaving seemed no more heart-wrenching than mine. She neither questioned her departure nor showed sadness or anger. For her, our household had furnished her with a shelter in the big city, far away from her marginal childhood in Königsberg. My mother's excellent recommendation attested to her many talents as cook and housekeeper, love of children and to her good natured and adaptable personality. She was certain of prompt reemployment. This time, she would work in a proper Aryan family.

MARIANNE
APRIL 1928

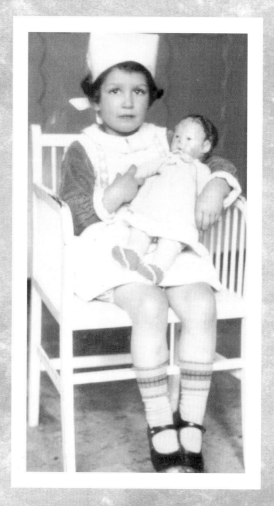

MARIANNE, WEARING A BABY NURSE CAP, TENDS
TO *HERMIE*, HER KÄTE KRUSE DOLL, 1928.

CHAPTER 5
THE YELLOW ROOM

My room was my anchor. It was not a large room, probably half the size of my brother's room. Yet, for me, it represented a known space where, behind closed doors, I felt safe from the outside world. The walls

HERMIE
IN A WICKER
DOLL CARRIAGE

of my room were painted with wide bands of yellow, deeper at the bottom, and almost transparent near the ceiling. My yellow room emanated a brightness and luminosity which, with the exception of my mother's dressing room, was not found anywhere else in the apartment.

Notwithstanding the ambiguous quality of my relationship with my mother, I imagined myself the preferred child because of that shared luminosity in our almost adjoining rooms.

During my eight years in the yellow room, none of the furniture changed, except for an adult-size bed that appeared on my eighth birthday, surprising me on my return from school. I loved its white simplicity and fresh look, its streamlined metal piping around the edges of the head and foot boards. The hard mattress took getting used to after years in my cuddly, sloppy, lived-in child's bed.

The straightforward, angular, pine cabinet was new, and painted in glossy white. Its shelves displayed neatly stacked underwear, shirts and sweaters. The other pieces of furniture, the bed-side table and the wardrobe, were antiques from Görlitz.

Over decades, the oak bedside table had been painted white to match the cabinet. It had faithfully discharged many functions before becoming mine. I was told it used to be in my grandparents' maid's room. The bottom section consisted of a box-like space whose small door concealed the ever-present chamber pot. On its top rested toys, dolls, or books, depending on my interest and age. Four spindle-like newels, about one and a half inches wide and four inches high, supported a narrow knobbed drawer, which contained my unassuming jewelry collection. Small necklaces, rings and bracelets, a mélange of glass beads, corals, and the currently fashionable squares of tiny colored beads filled the space. All these modest items lay tucked away in the night-table drawer during the week. Like medals of honor or crown jewels that never leave their velvety cases except for special state occasions, my finery could be worn only weekends and holidays, lest their frequent use would make me vain.

My mother must have considered pins and brooches less prone to induce vanity, since she permitted me to wear them whenever I wished. Depending on whim, I might adorn a sweater or dress with either of the two scotch terriers, one black, one white; a silver pin with two crossed skis, and the words *Ski Heil* printed at the crossing in small red letters; or a white Edelweiss, fashioned from an elephant's tooth. These riches were gifts from my parents' friends or souvenirs from summer vacations.

On occasions when I particularly pleased my mother, when I was the obedient child who anticipated her moods and wishes, when I laughed at her jokes and listened attentively to her comments and judgments, I would find a piece of candy on the Görlitz bedside table. It served to reward me for being her approving ally, and to encourage sweet dreams.

During my frequent bouts with the flu, the small square table top would be cluttered with Pyramidon (the German equivalent for aspirin), paper dolls, playing cards, my crochet hook with yarn, and the thermometer in a narrow purple case with which my mother, with obsessional regularity, checked my temperature.

My mother was at her best during my illnesses. At such times, she hovered over me with a care and concern that seemed excessive, but comforting. Memories of Valli's untimely death must have flooded her with thoughts of life's fragility. She stayed glued to my room, told me stories, read books, and watched me play with the cut-out dolls she had asked Fräulein Herta to buy for me. Her brittle remoteness gave way to a softness and warmth that I treasured.

Once my health was restored, my mother reverted to her customary remoteness, and my bedside table went back

BE OBEDIENT, BE MODEST,
GLADLY LISTEN TO YOUR PARENT'S ADVICE.
LEARN TO SPEAK, LEARN TO BE QUIET,
BUT ALWAYS AT THE PROPER TIME!

IN REMEMBRANCE OF

YOUR KÄTE
OCTOBER 8, 1935

to its uncluttered condition. As I became increasingly proficient in reading, a black gooseneck lamp towered over my bed. The rule was "Lights Out at Eight." Still, many were the evenings that my right hand cradled a book while my left thumb and index finger juggled the light switch, ready to turn it off with the approach of familiar footsteps.

Sometimes the black lamp was surrounded by a small fluted blue vase filled with wild-flowers from the Preussen Park. Multi-colored primroses, with yellow-like centers, filled the vase on April 19, my birthday.

The Görlitz table had a life of its own and was always ready to oblige my needs of the moment. Its top and its drawer, like all the drawers and doors of my room, provided me with a sense of power and control. I was chatelaine of my kingdom and could open and close drawers at will, lock and hide keys to protect my space from invasion or prying.

The bottom of my rectangular cabinet became the hiding place for the rolls of milk chocolate in their mauve Caillier wrapping that my parents brought back from annual trips to Switzerland. They were my very favorite chocolates, which I refused to share with anyone. Even their silver under-wrapping appealed to me. Long before aluminum foil became a household item, I revelled in its sparkle, forming scraps into a silver ball which I would hide with other treasurers in the cavernous depth of the white cabinet. Tightly locked, its key would be placed on the ledge of the armoire where it could be reached only by standing on my bed, stretching high.

The cause for these precautions was the snooping of my little brother, whose pilfering expeditions from his quarters at the other end of the apartment had increased over the years. A doll bed that fit snugly into the corner of the armoire's left side, where it would be out of view with the opening of the door, contained two or three dolls, dressed for bed, and covered by a short quilt. Hermine (Hermie for

MARIANNE'S DOLLS: *CHARLOTTE*, *DR. ROSENBERG* (A PINK DOG), AND *HERMIE*

short), a Käte Kruse doll, had been a gift from Onkel Herman on my first birthday. This doll was considered special on account of its simplicity in design. Its creator sewed it by hand out of soft materials and painted the face and the hair so as to approximate a child-like look. Hermie wore a white night-shirt with hand-made buttons and scalloped edges, part of her original wardrobe designed and sewn by Frau Lange from Görlitz. Beside her rested Charlotte, a flouncy doll in frilly pajamas, a strange contrast to the hairless, painted Hermie. Next to Hermie and Charlotte sat a soft pink dog named Dr. Rosenberg, and a small black baby doll, made of chocolate, and wrapped in colored metallic paper.

I must have neglected my charges for some time. But one rainy afternoon, as I removed the quilt to dress my dolls for an imaginary outing, I stared in utter disbelief. All that was left of the chocolate doll was its head. My mother and Fräulein Herta had to restrain my violent attack on my little brother, even though I knew my rage would hardly win the return of the black doll. I threw the remains of its head on his bed and locked myself into my room. As if to relieve my pain, on top of the Görlitz table at bedtime that night rested a glass bowl filled with my favorite marzipan potatoes from Hamann.

Like the night table, the Görlitz armoire had a special mystique having been in my mother's childhood room in the Bautzener Strasse. Now it stood at the foot of my bed, its scalloped panels and vaulted top casting a spooky silhouette against the wall and ceiling. I never felt quite at ease with this armoire. Its length and height were too prominent for my snug room, its narrow width made hanging clothes a continuous struggle, and its key needed an extra firm hand to shut the double doors. I often wondered how that tight space held my mother's long lace-embroidered gowns so heavily starched that they could stand on their own. What marvels of attention to detail those dresses must have been! My small cotton frocks suspended on their child-size hangers seemed altogether unworthy to occupy that space.

MARIANNE'S BIRTHDAY 1929
FEATURING A BUNDT CAKE AND THE FAMOUS CHOCOLATE DOLL

However, there were exceptions. I, too, had special dresses in soft cotton with paisley designs, heavily smocked across the top and around the puffed sleeves. They were sewn for me by Frau Kralert, a fleshy version of old Frau Zeck.

Frau Kralert's visits were a monthly occurrence. The sewing machine was set up in my brother's room. With her spidery, heavily-veined hands holding down the fabric, and her foot briskly rocking the treadle, she repaired torn sheets, patched my brother's pants, and stitched my summer and winter dresses.

Looking at those dresses, with their matching underpants and small draw string bags, hanging in orderly rows in the armoire, I made up stories of rearranging them in a children's specialty store where I imagined working as an elegant sales lady with high heels, black silk stockings with a thick black seam down the back of the leg, dark red nail polish and lots of makeup. Being a sales lady sounded highly desirable.

On Sunday family walks, with stops at a café, or at birthday parties, I considered myself the best-dressed child. Yet these moments of narcissistic fancy did not make me feel happy. The first six years of my life were devoid of even the most fleeting connection with other children, except for my brother. Dedda, his nurse, with her white starched uniform, her pale face and cold hands, and my brother in the carriage or playpen, were my only companions, not counting my dolls and stuffed animals.

No wonder that the first birthday party to which I was invited, at age six, at the opulent Kurfürstendamm apartment of my classmate, Dorchen Oppenheim, resulted in a nightmare for me, and in an embarrassment for my mother. I did not know how to behave. I could not remain seated, polite and well-mannered, around the festively arranged table along side the other little girls in their pretty smocked dresses. I did not know what to say or what to do. Frantically,

I rushed in relief to the door each time the bell rang, until my mother at last appeared and rescued me from this torture.

Back at our apartment, I rampaged through the entry hall, looking neither right nor left. All I wanted was to hide in my room. I still had to reach the back hall, lined with shelved closets, where my mother kept the linen. Yet, once back in my safe place with its peaceful view on the blooming acacia tree, I felt as if I had escaped from an indescribable danger. I found solace in this familiar solitude close to my parents' bedroom, with its terrace, its geranium planters and the winter locker for the Danish butter.

In my room, I inhabited a different world from that of my little brother, Fräulein Herta and Tante Toni. Their rooms were at a sharp right turn from the entry hall, away from the rest of the apartment. They looked down on the busy traffic of Brandenburgische Strasse. I gazed out on gardens, trees and attractive houses and villas, away from the hum of the city. I could see birds nesting in the acacia tree and felt safe in the proximity of my parents' quarters.

Ours was a typical Berlin apartment, with its long, dark, labyrinthine corridors and its many doors always solidly shut with German thoroughness. A curtained glass door on the right opened from the entry hall onto the living room, the *Herrenzimmer*. The living and dining rooms were connected by glass-panelled doors whose curtains matched the green raw silk on the other doors. The dining room was similar in size to the living room. It also faced Ravensberger Strasse and opened to the small hall that contained the wall telephone, the bell register, the kitchen entrance and, ultimately, the back door to Else's quarters.

To burst into a room without knocking was strictly forbidden to my brother and me. Only the bathroom could be entered without such formality, since it was locked when in use. One bathroom, with tub, bidet, two sinks (set in black-and-white marble), and toilet, sufficed for our household of seven. On the left, off the entry hall, nestled a tiny lavatory, with a minute washbasin. As was customary in Berlin apartments, washbasins with warm and cold running water were installed in some of the bedrooms, including mine and the one shared by my brother and Fräulein Herta. Since we rarely took showers or baths, the basins sufficed for sponge baths and the brushing of teeth. Tante Toni and Else, by contrast, were required to carry pitchers of water into their rooms for their daily toilet. In housecoat and slippers, unkempt and barely awake, they made their way to the lavatory each morning, chamber pot in hand.

My parents and I used chamber pots as well. Mine was made out of white metal with a narrow black rim and a shiny black handle. Upside down, it looked like a hat, and was well hidden in the bottom of the Görlitz bedside table. My parents' chamber pots, by contrast, were voluptuously curved vessels of heavy buff porcelain splendor which seemed worthy of much loftier usage.

The only time that my chamber pot became a source of embarrassment was when my mother insisted on taking it on our summer vacation to Heringsdorf on the Baltic, when I was six. Since no one could shake my mother's conviction that hotel lavatories were carriers of unmentionable diseases, I was forced to walk to the bathroom down the hall, my metal pot furtively hidden under my red-and-white polka-dotted terry cloth beach wrap. Two future classmates in first grade who were staying at the same hotel would never have ceased to tease me, had they noticed.

At home, I can't remember Fräulein Herta, Tante Toni or Else ever luxuriating in the splendor of the deep, marble ensconced bathtub next to my room. I do, however, remember my little brother during his occasional bath, surrounded by small sailboats, rubber ducks and fishes, as he was shampooed and scrubbed by our devoted Kinderfräulein.

Occasionally, I kept my mother company while she took her bath. I would sit on the edge of the bidet whose real function puzzled me. With a snicker, my brother and I referred to this mysterious fixture as *Popo Badewanne* . It's sole function for me was to soak my toes in a heavy solution of tincture of benzoid when suffering from frostbites following an afternoon of ice skating. My mother's bath seemed to consist of an extraordinarily long soak in foamy bubbles, which would separate long enough to permit the surfacing of two sizable bosoms that floated up and down as if they were unattached and had lives of their own. Either Else or Fräulein Herta appeared toward the end of her bath, placed a large towel over her shoulders, and blotted my mother dry.

The wall behind the two large washbasins was lined with a long mirror at which I loved to cast furtive glances, obviously to admire myself. "Marianne, don't be *eitel*," was my mother's continuous reprimand. If I seemed to like my looks, I was *eitel*. If I put on airs, I was *eitel*. If I looked longingly at myself in the mirror, I was *eitel*. Vain comes close to its meaning but does not capture it completely. Yet my mother did promote my orthodonture. Where was the dividing line?

I don't recollect that anyone else in my class wore braces. While some of my classmates could have benefited from orthodonture, it was as yet rare, and generally considered extravagant and vain. Why tamper with what God had given us? My parents had no such scruples, and rather welcomed the chance to obliterate blemishes. They welcomed these advances in dentistry in their single-minded wish to fashion a daughter as perfect as possible. The future embraced those endowed with beauty and talent, qualities my parents hoped to cultivate in me. Yet, at the same time, my mother faulted me for being *eitel*.

"Enough now of looking at yourself, Marianne,"

admonished my mother. "Fräulein Herta will cover your mirror with newspaper. That'll teach you not to look at yourself all the time."

The newspaper-taped mirror, which hung above my small porcelain sink where I brushed my teeth and attended to my rudimentary toilet, became a source of contemptuous hilarity to Reni and Elisabeth. "How can you let your mother do that to you?" they asked mockingly.

Unequivocal loyalty to my mother ("Never soil your own nest," as my father would say), and embarrassment at my obvious docility (I never fought back), made me minimize this personal indignity. "Who needs a mirror?" I lied.

Yet, one day, even I lost my accustomed docility. Else had the afternoon off. Fräulein Herta was somewhere with my brother, and my mother was on her usual shopping expedition. I was alone in the apartment.

In my mother's dressing room, the sun sparkled through the windows. A mild spring breeze billowed the loosely woven curtains and the pungent scent of acacia blossoms permeated the room. The silver filigree around the edges of the closet doors and the matching marble table glittered in the light.

I sat in front of the three-way mirror. "Mirror, mirror on the wall, what can you tell me about the future?" I was handsome enough, according to the mirror. What fun to be a girl! The fresh spring breeze seemed to blow an unfamiliar, momentary excitement through me as well. For once, I did not feel empty. I felt adventurous. Is that what my mother feared from the mirror?

Boldly, I began to try on her hats neatly arranged on off-yellow eight-inch stands, designed for that purpose, in her built-in closet. All her hats were made to order, with the designer's label neatly sewn in the interior. The hat I loved the most was not an important felt one, with wide rim and grosgrain ribbon. My favorite was a little black cap of metallic thread that tilted slightly over the right ear, leaving the left ear exposed. A narrow glass bar, encased in a silver mold, fastened the cap to the hair.

I picked out a scarf from the many drawers, some of which contained my mother's pink silk underwear, her corsets and brassieres, all neatly arranged and delicately scented with Chanel #5™.

This was fun. Behind the mirror doors, I inspected my mother's array of makeup. The orange, white and black Coty™ powder box, with its swansdown puff and delicately

1930 OIL PAINTING OF MARIANNE HOLDING BALL

BY BERLIN ARTIST GRAUMAN

perfumed scent, bewitched me. An oval crystal dish contained her lipsticks. The well-used mascara slate, hard as a rock, caught my attention. Having often watched my mother apply her mascara, I now used my spittle to moisten the brush, and rubbed it as forcibly as I could on the coal-black surface, trying to make it stick. Carefully I blackened my lashes, rouged my cheeks, powdered my nose and applied a bright-red lipstick. I saw myself transformed into a clown, a person I did not recognize and did not especially like. Obviously, more finesse would be needed in the future to enhance and embellish. Satisfied that my experimentation was at an end, I looked for the cleansing cream. At that moment, my mother appeared at the door. She stopped short in disbelief. She saw before her a potential harlot on a fast-track into the gutter.

"What are you doing?" she shouted, her cheeks crimson. She pulled me by the hair, shook me hard and slapped me with both hands. Her face was contorted, her eyes seemingly receded into their sockets. "You'll end up like those girls on the Oranienburger Strasse, mark my words."

Never before had I seen my mother that enraged and out of control. To me, it was both incomprehensible and frightening. Without putting anything back in order, I made my escape. Safely between my four walls, I rubbed off the remaining makeup with the all-purpose vaseline, puzzled and stunned, but not guilty. I had done nothing wrong.

I knew my mother's rage would subside. But, first she would appear at the dinner table with a freezing look, then ignore me for the next few days, until I apologized. For what?

On days when my mother's rage was apparent to everyone in the household, Tante Toni, Fräulein Herta or Else would drop in to my room to chat. No such compassion emanated from my brother. He was gloating.

During one of those times of my mother's neglect, I was overcome by that familiar feeling of emptiness and boredom.

Near the telephone, I came across a box of kitchen matches which Else used to light the gas stove. They responded to my craving for action. A small strike and there was light. What power I suddenly had! I was entranced by the flickering flame which reminded me of my birthday candles in the wooden hand-painted Swedish ring, and of the magic of candles at Christmas and Chanukkah. I had not meant to set a fire, but the more I struck matches, the more I needed to continue. Inertia had ended.

The smell of my spirited animations began to permeate the rest of the apartment. The kitchen door opened, creating a sudden draft. My match dropped into the wastebasket and ignited the paper. We had a fire, set by Marianne. General havoc ensued. My already incited mother dug her nails into my skin. "Go to your room, and don't come out until I call you," she hissed, convinced that her reasonable child had become a pyromaniac.

My mother was puzzling. On one hand, she maintained an iron control over almost every aspect of my life. On the other hand, she permitted me to bicycle on my own through the heavy traffic of central Berlin. Apart from the unruly traffic, I was accosted by boys and men who whistled, trailed me and engaged me in dubious conversation. Successful in escaping, I got home breathless but elated at having eluded these street hazards. I rather delighted in those moments of danger, in my ability to cope. I never mentioned these incidents to anyone.

My mother controlled, but not coddled. She was a proponent of the stiff upper lip. "Don't act like a child, Marianne," she chided whenever I was sad, angry, jealous, or when I cried. "Be reasonable, good, well-behaved."

Much like my grandfather Alexander, my mother was the only person in the household with the right to openly express anger and disapproval. Once when I complained to the governess of a playmate that my mother never kept her promises, she refused to look at me or talk to me for a week, until again I apologized.

Only once do I remember my father's fury. He tore a wreath of daisies out of my hair when, after having bitten my nails, I had developed a blood infection and required surgery. My brother, on the other hand, was a more frequent victim of his occasional outbursts, which I witnessed in helpless consternation. This seemed odd in view of the fact that he had desperately wanted a son and, as my mother told me, was dismayed when his first child was girl.

"Children are like dogs, and dogs belong under the table," was one of my father's familiar refrains. To this he added with patriarchal satisfaction, "In our household prevails a harsh but loving tone."

Well, maybe. It was Passover again, and I, an eight-year-old, discovered the hidden Matzo, and as a reward could wish for anything I desired. That year I yearned for a puppy. My parents smiled knowingly and sent my brother and me to the post office, a block away at the corner of Wittelsbacher Strasse, where a puppy would be waiting for us. In our shared desire for a dog, we held hands as we marched, hopefully, toward our destination.

We arrived at the Post Office, but the black iron grill of the door was firmly locked. The Post Office was closed. We looked at one another, speechless. How could our parents inflict a cruel joke like that on us! We were united in disbelief and fury. Our parents had made us the innocent victims of that raw, sadistic and bizarre sense of humor, the famous *Berliner Witz*. I felt ridiculous for not having realized that it was after-hours, and of course, the Post Office would be closed.

A dog finally materialized, in the form of a soft white toy terrier, with a red leather collar, a small bell, and a red coat. He joined my other animals and dolls and was named Freddy. Conceived in such pain, he became my favorite mascot. He was equally appreciated by Peter, the son of Alfred Silberstein, my father's partner, and Lutz Moos, a snotty, feisty, yet funny boy, the son of another one of my parents' friends. They invented games, involving Freddy and the rest of my menagerie. Barking like lunatics and on all fours, they navigated my stuffed animals through the never-ending corridors of our serpentine apartment, and momentarily treated me as their equal. I was ten and they were twelve. The complicity was fleeting and soon they were back to their habitual teasing and torturing that drove me to tears.

Was sich neckt, das liebt sich (You tease who you love), consoled Tante Toni when I sought solace in her tasseled room. Sure, I had a crush on both of them, changing my preference from day to day. Merely to be noticed by them, I would gladly part with my favorite pencils, yo-yos, or marbles. Yet none my sacrificial offerings accomplished the desired goal. In their eyes, I remained a second-class citizen.

It was during one of my frequent visits to the Silbersteins' fancy apartment on Helmstädter Strasse that Peter's mother, Grete, a coquettish dark brunette, inquired whether I were in love with her son. Of course not, I countered. She then proceeded to quiz me as to whether I were already *aufgeklärt*, literally meaning enlightened, but referring to knowing the facts of life. She relished sexual innuendos and enjoyed holding my mother's reticence in matters of sex up to ridicule. Having teased me into admitting that indeed I had not been *aufgeklärt*, she quickly dropped the subject and assured me that one of these days my mother would clue me in.

And indeed she did when, at the age of twelve, I started my period. At that point, my mother had no choice but to initiate me into the monthly phenomenon that signified my passage into womanhood. All I remember about her awkward and laborious explanation was a list of words: unfertilized eggs, twenty-eight days, cramps and a lengthy sermon to take especially good care of myself at those times. Tante Regi, a distant cousin of my father and the family beauty, was famous for staying in bed the entire week. Ostensibly, that week of enforced rest accounted for her undiminished beauty until her death at age eighty-five.

Relieved in having discharged her duty, my mother rang the bell for Fräulein Herta and dispatched her to purchase the required paraphernalia.

"And now you can be excused from gym," added Tante Toni with a grin.

Why had I never put two and two together when increasing numbers of my classmates were excused from our biweekly gym classes upon presentation of a small blue notebook? No climbing bars, no long jumps, no rings.

Now I, too, had arrived. With joy I was greeted by my already initiated sisterhood. The fact that I was Jewish seemed not to matter. Barbara, Frederike and Christine were on the sidelines that particular day. Usually they ignored me or, if need be, exchanged but the most sparing of words. Their eyes lit up. Clutching my arms, they invited me to sit between them. "Now you're just like us," they beamed.

This initiation seemed to coincide with my awakening from a long slumber. Not long afterwards, Rudi, a distant cousin from Dresden, moved to Berlin with his parents, on their way to Holland. Persecuted by the Nazis, Rudi's father was forced to liquidate his dental practice. During his brief stay in Berlin the summer of 1937, Rudi became a frequent visitor and, to my amazement, seemed to like me. Maybe I was not as undesirable as Peter and Lutz made me feel. At fourteen, Rudi towered over me, at least a head. I was admiringly aware of his strong arms and shoulders, and his good-natured face which looked at me approvingly. His shorts exposed the muscular legs with which he took giant steps that left me trailing behind. He invited me to my favorite ice cream parlor at Olivaer Platz and taught me to play tennis.

Then he came to say good-bye. He squeezed next to me at my old-fashioned desk. Its bench and table were of one piece, and I had to slip in from the left because the large curve on the right, for raising the top and leaning my arm on, left little space.

The desk had seemed enormous when it arrived in 1930, along with the *Zuckertuete*, the large, painted, papier-mâché cone, filled with sweets that was given to German children on their first day of school, to funnel into their heads a love of learning.

At this desk, I formed my first letters, my first numbers, drew pictures for school or for special birthdays. Here I did my homework for history, geography, and geometry, or worked on my modest stamp collection. Here I wrote in my diary or just sat and stared into the acacia tree, but always alone.

Now Rudi shared my private space and told me that he loved me. His arm hugged my shoulder as he awkwardly planted a kiss on my cheek. I drew back, embarrassed, confused. Rudi had become my buddy, my friend. I felt nothing else. In spite of my struggles, I still preferred Peter and Lutz who challenged me.

Rudi's departure, after a courteous leave-taking with my mother, was a relief.

"What's the matter, Marianne? You seem troubled," observed my mother, with rare insight.

"Rudi told me that he loves me," I muttered, still puzzled by his declaration.

My mother laughed. "Prepare yourself," she said. "This will not be the last time. There will be others. But Rudi is a nice boy."

Her unaccustomed lightheartedness disturbed me and did nothing to reduce my confusion. But by now, I knew better than to expect useful responses. I forgave her and dealt

MARIANNE, PETER AND HANS 1936

with this new world of feelings on my own.

Rudi's frequent and lengthy letters made little impression on me. A snap-shot showing him older and taller, still in leather shorts, held no interest for me. I stopped answering his letters.

If those walls could have talked, they would have told a mixed tale. Yes, there were joys, and moments of rare excitement. Looking out on the acacias, or divining the weather from the reflection of the sun on a neighboring house, were unique pleasures. But my walls largely compressed the tensions and uncertainties of growing up in a world that contained few answers, and in which those that were offered made little sense.

Fräulein Herta 1934

CHAPTER 6
FRÄULEIN HERTA

Else's leaving, as ordained by the Nüremberg Laws, was an accomplished fact that I had simply accepted. By contrast, Fräulein Herta's departure in the spring of 1937 affected me with a deep sense of loss. Desolate, I crouched on her bed in the room she shared with my brother, and watched her pack.

FRÄULEIN HERTA, HANS, PETER, MARIANNE, JULIAN AND ERNA

What would life be like without her? One of her suitcases was open, while another, nearly full, lay on the table in the room's alcove. The doors and drawers of the built-in closets along the entire wall were ajar as Fräulein Herta removed her blouses, dresses, sweaters, and lingerie. A whiff of her singular scent, a mixture of a delicate sweetish powder and perspiration, filled the air.

I loved the buttons that decorated her tightly fitting sweaters. With her small bust, these sweaters, worn over long, smoothly fitting skirts, made her look taller and thinner than she actually was. Her slim neck gave way to a finely chiseled round face which, accentuated by sad and searching eyes, always gazed gently at me. She wore her straight dark hair in a bob, parted on the left side, slightly covering her ears and the frames of her black-rimmed glasses.

Over the several previous Sundays, Fräulein Herta's father had made the one-and-a-half hour train trip from his suburban home in Pankow to our apartment in Wilmersdorf to help move the many belongings his daughter had accumulated over these seven years as our Kinderfräulein. The suitcases that Herr Plew carried away contained photo albums of summer trips to Spindlermühl, Obersdorf, the Baltic and the North Sea. They burst at the seams with the many gifts from my parents: purses, scarves, nightgowns, crockery, and handkerchiefs and doilies embroidered by me behind the locked doors of my yellow sanctuary for her birthdays or for Christmas.

Fräulein Herta had arrived with our move to Brandenburgische Strasse, with Else, and with my entering first grade at age six. My little brother was almost three. At that time, we had outgrown the nurse Dedda, who was hired to take care of the two of us shortly after my brother's birth. I could not have been more delighted and relieved at her departure. Her pasty, tight-lipped face with beady gray eyes, and her stringy dull blond hair, invariably crowned by a

HANS,
NURSE DEDDA
AND MARIANNE
1928

starched nurse's cap, rarely looked with kindness upon me. Her equally starched white uniform and apron emitted a coldness I feel in my bones even now. That uniform was such a part of her presence, that I failed to recognize her in ordinary clothes on her afternoons off.

No doubt my simmering resentment was due to her obvious preference for my brother. After all, he was *her* baby, just as I had once been Taute's baby. Taute had been present at my birth and had taken care of me with undivided and adoring attention, along with Anna from Görlitz, until the arrival of the new baby. She indulged me lovingly. No wonder I resented being second.

Old photographs confirm that Taute, a rotund woman in her early fifties, looks cheerful and satisfied with life as she sits on a park bench in the *Tiergarten* with my mother, and me, the baby, in a huge black baby carriage. A similar photo a few years later shows a pinched, dissatisfied Dedda, my mother, a grouchy three-and-half-year old me and now my little brother in the same black, cavernous carriage. Taute was happily married and had children of her own. Dedda, by contrast, had to support her elderly mother and crippled father, and spent her days off taking care of them. Of course she was bitter, but why had my mother hired her?

It was a foregone conclusion that my mother would engage baby nurses, and later on, governesses, to look after us. In Dedda, she had found an efficient and hygienic helper who carried out her commands without a moment's hesitation. My pleading "It's stopped raining, I don't need galoshes," would be countered by "But Mutti wants you to." The two women harmonized in their readiness to deny and withhold.

In relinquishing her maternal responsibilities to Fräulein Herta, my mother created a scenario in which I fared much better. While my beloved Fräulein Herta would not venture dramatically from my mother's prescribed course, she nonetheless exercised sound and fair judgment and often mitigated my mother's rigid or thoughtless positions. Thanks to Fräulein Herta, I could exchange my bulky winter knee-highs for anklets and shed my heavy sweaters not too long after my less-pampered classmates had already made that switch.

When I was eight, my mother decided to send me to Major Böhmer's weekly gymnastic classes, which I anticipated with unmitigated horror. I considered myself the clumsiest and most unattractive child in the class. While all the other girls, tall or short, slim or chubby, blond or brunette, skipped around in the prettiest of light-blue, pink or lavender satin underpants, I lumbered along in heavy white cotton briefs. The forty-five minute walk to Major Böhmer's was always a nightmare. With no joy in sight, the long and arduous walk took us first along Wilmersdorf Strasse, then on Bismarck Strasse along low wrought iron fences that enclosed small areas of grass designed to distance the apartment houses from direct contact with the street was a nightmare. Fräulein Herta noticed my bad temper, but could not guess the reason. I wanted satin underpants!

Major Böhmer, a retired army officer well known to a certain Berlin social set, cleared his huge dining room of all its furniture to hold classes. There he would teach barefoot and bare chested prepubescent girls good posture, nimbleness of movement and lightness of gait. Long-haired or short-haired, we paraded around the room on polished hardwood floors, to the sound of German marches and the major's verbal assault on our lack of decorum and single mindedness of purpose. The ever-watchful and approving mothers and governesses, patiently awaiting the end of the hour on hard folding chairs along the walls, were equally admonished for chatting or laughing with Major Böhmer's tight-lipped reprimand. The chatter stopped. The unheated staircases were cold during Berlin winters.

Even today, the sounds of the Radetski March transport me back to those unfriendly, martial afternoons where I suffered the rigors and commands of the major, the chagrin of not having the proper attire, and the estrangement from all those little girls who seemed carefree and self-confident, wearing their shiny underpants with such ease. Whether they knew each other or not, they carried on a continuous hum of chatter, whispers, and giggles, but not with me. What could they be saying to one another? Why was it so hard to be included? To the bulky weight of my cotton pants was added the paralysis in my throat. Only the most banal and maladroit words came out. My world seemed all darkness and frustration; theirs, all lightness and joy.

I don't believe that I was ever asked whether I enjoyed Major Böhmer's classes. It was merely good for me. There were moments when I fantasized about ballet classes, satin slippers, frilly tutus, ribbons in my hair. For my mother, such affectations were suspect. Her strident walk in her sturdy shoes and severely tailored suits (what a change from the elegant frocks and shoes of her Danzig days) matched the major's rigorous approach. The more graceful and delicate movements of ballet would have left her uneasy. Frivolity went against her character.

Julian and Erna 1937

Steadfastly prodding me to reveal the cause of my obvious distress, Fräulein Herta finally untangled its roots. Somehow, she must have described my dilemma in sufficiently compelling terms, since my mother eventually granted my wish and I, too, donned those highly desirable satin pants, and even began to make friends.

Walks of a happier nature with Fräulein Herta were to swimming lessons at Halensee, one of Berlin's many lakes and a favorite recreation area for all ages. A streetcar ride of five stops from our apartment, we were, however, required to walk since, of course, walking was good for us! Sometimes accompanied by my brother, Fräulein Herta and I walked up Westphälische Strasse to Ku-Damm until it became Königs Allee where an insignificant entrance paved the way to a long downhill walk that led to the lake and pools. At the entrance, we were greeted by a chubby, bouncy woman whose keys jingled on a belt around her waist. With one of them, she opened a cabin in the woman's section on the left where we changed and hung up our street clothes. The cost of the cabin depended on the length of our stay.

From early June, in cool weather, or even in rain, I passed through the various stages of expertise in swimming. "Don't be a sissy," droned the swimming teacher as my teeth chattered and my body shivered. "Keep moving and you'll get warm."

And move I did. At the outset, with a six-inch-wide cork belt around my chest, I paddled in the shallowest lake-fed pool of water, separated from the lake only by the rectangle of changing cabins. Our broad-shouldered swimming instructor practiced what he preached. Indeed, he was *abgehärtet* (toughened to the elements), and wore nothing but swimming trunks even in the coldest weather. I remember looking up from the water and seeing his trunk-like legs as my eyes followed him along the wooden walk, trailing a large bamboo stick for me to grasp when frightened.

Once I graduated from the intermediate pool, the expanse of the lake, surrounded by trees and villas in the distance, became my summer playground. In the period of three years, a sizeable group of us moved from novices to *Freischwimmer* (free swimming for fifteen minutes) onto the category of *Fahrtenschwimmer* (free swimming for forty-five minutes). We were an ambitious lot. Some of us dived off the springboards elegantly piercing the water like well-aimed arrows. Others, with fingers pinching their nostrils shut, crashed like sacks of potatoes into the water. I never did reach *Totenkopf*, (one and a half hour of uninterrupted swimming), the highest category.

Annual snapshots of me in swimming suits show my changing contours, which coincided with mother's permission for me to ride my well-polished Dunlop bicycle to Halensee alone. I would have died rather than admit to my dread of those solo jaunts, and my anxious search for companions once I arrived. Since none of my classmates went to Halensee, I attached myself to anyone who showed an interest in a stray young adolescent. I befriended a middle-aged sun bather and made myself useful by applying pungent coconut oil to her shoulders and legs. Turning from front to back, she would tell me how she needed an even tan for the décolleté dresses her husband liked on her. "In the summer I swim. In the winter I play bridge," she confided. "I don't want children. They'd be too much trouble." Compared with her, even my mother led a more useful life.

At other times, I joined a group of older girls who were tolerant of a lone and curious child. I had nothing to say to them, but eavesdropped with fascination on their talk about movies, boys and parents. They let me swim with them and included me in their races to the life buoys at the far end of the lake. They adopted me. They fussed over me, combed my curly hair into new styles, and treated me to lemonade. In turn, I was their devoted slave, full of admiration for their apparent sophistication. I willingly delivered messages to some youths across the deck, and fetched dry towels from their cabins. Notwithstanding the initial anxiety that had accompanied these trips, once I had established my connection with these girls, my hours at Halensee became pleasurable events. I kept up my regular visits until one day the sign "Juden nicht erwünscht" (Jews are not welcome) prominently greeted me at the entrance.

Long before I was permitted to take off on my own, Fräulein Herta was the most important person in my life. In the mornings, it was she who opened my shutters and curtains.

"Time to get up, start getting dressed and come to breakfast," she called in her low voice. Else served me

USCHI, HANS AND MARIANNE AT THE HALENSEE (SWIM CLUB)
1935

breakfast at the white kitchen table. Invariably, the Dresden onion-pattern cup, filled to the brim with café au lait, was sitting beside the daily buttered hard roll that, still warm, had just been delivered. I accepted the roll without great relish. It merely served to stem my hunger. I was given the choice of butter or jam. Both together would have been excessive.

Less spartan breakfasts lingered in my memory. I was very young, having breakfast with my father in the dining room at Tielewardenberg Strasse. The table was set with a thickly embroidered cotton tablecloth in red, black and white geometric patterns, no doubt Frau Lange's handiwork. My father, with his housejacket, and pomaded hair, removed the three-and-a-half-minute egg from the round egg basket, whose top and sides flounced in yellow crochets. With a sharp knife, he cut the tip of the egg now nestled in its sparkling silver egg cup. I awaited the magic word that broke the silence. "Motte, how about the tip of the egg?" A dab of butter and a dash of salt went on the cut-off top, which was gently guided into my mouth with a silver egg spoon. Quietly, I watched as my father read the *Berliner Tageblatt*. I waited for him to remove the soft part from his roll. He ate only the crust. The soft part was *fuer die Voegel*, for the birds. I was one of those little birds, and I was happy.

Breakfast later by myself in the kitchen was something to endure and to escape from quickly. The kitchen walls, the cupboards, the chairs and table were scrubbed shiny, clear white, cold and aseptic like Dedda's uniform. The kitchen took on an inviting aura only when Else's family sat around the table and I could listen to their gossip and partake in their *Kaffee und Kuchen*.

That kitchen had other momentary thrills. I loved leafing through the few cookbooks hidden behind imposing cast-iron pots and pans on the bottom shelf. Were they concealed so as not to remind anyone as to what food, imaginatively

MARIANNE AND JULIAN SHARING BREAKFAST
AT TIELEWARDENBERG STRASSE, 1925

and beautifully prepared, could look like, or for that matter, taste like? Our daily fare was a far cry from those enticing color photographs of salmon mousse; saffron rice covered with lobster, shrimp and crab; stuffed artichokes; parsleyed veal shanks in shiny brown sauce; or desserts from a strange Lucullan continent. Those magic pages made me momentarily forget the cold tiled floor, the sterile kitchen, and transported me to a land of fantasy and desire.

"Get your coat, Marianne, hurry, or you'll be late." Fräulein Herta summoned at the kitchen door. Off to school! I donned the wrap appropriate to the season and swung my brown leather back-pack, the indispensable *Tornister*, across my shoulders. A small bag, dangling on narrow leather straps from neck to waist, contained the sandwich and fruit I would eat at our ten o'clock recess.

Both bags gave way to the longed-for grown-up carrying bag once I moved on to the Lyzeum. Since this important purchase symbolized my growing up, it had to meet all my requirements in terms of elegance, size, texture and smell. My father made time to shop with me *Unter den Linden*, in one of the fancy leather shops. There was no vacillation in making the choice. I went straight to a medium-brown briefcase in calf leather with two large inside sections and two small pockets in the front. Two brass locks made a mellow sound when shut and the solid leather handle fit nicely in my grip.

During the four years at the private grade school run by the Misses Meyer, Fräulein Herta and I walked the twenty-five minute distance together four times a day. She would pick me up at noon for lunch and return me to school at two o'clock. The four years are compressed in my mind as one continuous walk from my house to school and back. Our route varied only slightly. Sometimes we passed the open-air market across the tennis courts on Zähringer Strasse, which in the winter months were flooded and were turned into the neighborhood ice-skating rink.

It was Fräulein Herta who accompanied me on my first visits to the rink on winter afternoons. She made sure my skates were securely fastened to my boots with the aid of the small metal key that resembled a miniature cork screw, and that I was properly settled in my skating class. Once I was older and more proficient, I set out on my own, warmly wrapped in navy-blue pants, matching jacket, and high laced boots, my skates held together with a leather strap that I carried over my shoulders, one skate dangling in front, the other in back. I skated around the rink, looking for someone to skate with. Occasionally another solitary girl or boy asked me to skate as a team. Arms linked, we tried out various patterns, figure eights, dances and jumps, moving close together then apart, to the waltzes or marches that drifted through the cold air from a small building at the entrance. That building served as ticket office and warm-up hut in the winter and tennis club in the summer. A small counter with hot chocolate, jelly-doughnuts, and candy attracted me like a magnet. Since my weekly allowance never exceeded ten

PREUSSEN PARK WINTER SCENE

pfennig, I was hard put to afford these small luxuries. I never stole, but I used ruses to obtain the necessary cash. Occasionally, Tante Toni accompanied me to the skating rink. With feigned dismay, I announced that, in the hurry of leaving, I had forgotten to ask Mutti for ticket money. Dutifully, my aunt searched her coin purse for the extra twenty-five pfennig, and, with nonchalant satisfaction, I was off to the counter for hot chocolate or a licorice roll. A small reserve even sufficed for future indulgence.

On my daily walks to school with Fräulein Herta, I used to linger, much to her displeasure, at the stationery store at the corner of Zähringer and Konstanzer Strasse. The display of fountain pens, crayons and multi-colored paper notebooks captivated me. I could almost smell the leather satchels in the show-case and feel their smooth surface. Another frequent stop was a hole-in-the-wall bakery, two steps off the street, in a dreary concrete apartment building on Düsseldorfer Strasse.

"Here comes the young Fräulein," was the baker's unfailing greeting. "And taller and more beautiful than the last time." I relished the flattery uttered in his broad Berlinese patois. I also loved his round face full of dimples and laugh lines, and his enormous beer belly which caused him considerable effort as he bent down for the big loaves of white rye that were his specialty, and the only bread we ever ate at home. The smell of the still-warm bread would accompany us all the way home while I chewed on the cookie the baker had handed me with admonition not to tell my mother.

Those walks with their sights and smells have remained with me more vividly than my four years at the Meyer school. I don't remember what or how I learned. Some preoccupation made that process difficult. However, I enjoyed writing the letters of the alphabet and the numbers (of which the number eight was my very favorite). I even enjoyed the early stages of math and geometry, but when it came to retaining miscellaneous and general information, I lost interest. Yet I must have absorbed enough rudimentary skills to have been admitted, in 1934, to the prestigious Hohenzollern Lyzeum. While many of my Jewish classmates continued at Jewish high schools, my father's service record of fighting for the Vaterland during the first World War facilitated my acceptance at the Lyzeum.

It was Fräulein Herta's presence that made the travels through my Berlin so pleasurable. With her I felt at one, whether we talked or whether we were silent. I believe that she loved me even though she never said so. Her lightness of spirit and her affection, support and encouragement made me feel less restless. Perhaps she saw in my tentative attempts to make sense of a puzzling world the struggles and frustrations she, too, had once experienced. But all this I only surmised. No matter how hard I tried, I never succeeded in eliciting facts about her early life, or, for that matter, her current one. All I knew was that before coming

1930s Berlin Storefronts

to us, she was a governess to some children in Turkey. I found myself wondering whether her charges in that far away land were more lovable than I.

Over the years, Fräulein Herta's parents became an important part of my life as they also considered my brother and me part of their family. Her father was a railroad official, and her mother, a jolly, plump housewife whose yeast cakes I adored and whose passion for gardening was for me an unfamiliar but highly impressive talent.

From time to time, on her Sunday afternoons off, Fräulein Herta invited my brother and me to her parents' Pankow bungalow. At the station Zoo, we caught the interurban train that would take us through grimy, gray neighborhoods of factories and run-down, crowded workers' apartments. Laundry of all shapes and colors fluttered from one window ledge to another, breaking the monotony and sadness of the buildings. An occasional advertisement, for the laundry soap Persil or for Bolle milk, flashed past as we made our way through a city I did not know. Soon, the squalor and oppression gave way to a friendly and inviting countryside, where neat, small houses, surrounded by fenced-in garden plots, revealed the vast diversity of Greater-Berlin.

Already at the Pankow station, I inhaled a different air. Depending on the time of year, I either breathed in the perfume of spring blossoms, jasmine, manure, hay, or the smoke of burning fall leaves. For seven years, I savored the changing seasons in the simple, warm presence of Fräulein Herta's easygoing family. There we talked about inconsequential things, laughed and played games. Life there seemed strangely carefree and simple.

Of all the seasons in the Plews' garden, it is autumn that still explodes fireworks of color in my mind. Large, staked orange, lemon, and red dahlias vied with multicolored zinnias, with yellow marigolds of all sizes, with the pastel shades of asters, and glowing nasturtiums, tomatoes, and green beans. An abundance of fruit, flowers and vegetables emanated from that small garden plot. Every inch was put to its best use. Apple and pear trees protected wax-like begonias from the sun and furnished shade for the round table and chairs, where, among this marvelous jungle of vegetation, coffee and a raisin yeast cake awaited our arrival.

As I grew older, these weekend excursions became less frequent, and on the occasions when we did visit, a tension had crept into the formerly happy and carefree atmosphere. No longer did we chat freely about the happenings on Brandenburgische Strasse, the exploits of Else and her family, or the comings and goings of my parents. Fräulein Herta became tongue-tied, her chatty and always interested mother appeared absent-minded, and her gentle and attentive father distanced himself to the corner chair and read the paper.

IN WERTE FOR THE CHERRY BLOSSOMS, SPRING, 1936, MARIANNE AND FRÄULEIN HERTA ARE ON THE FAR RIGHT.

Even at home, Fräulein Herta's usual calm demeanor had given way to an unaccustomed preoccupation. She had begun to receive phone calls that she would answer with obvious apprehension. Called to the phone by Anna, Else's more matronly replacement, she looked awkward and flushed.

One Wednesday afternoon as I returned from school, I encountered Fräulein Herta at the corner of our street greeting an attractive, sandy-haired man who clasped her hand tightly in his. As their eyes met, both of their faces lit up. I had never seen her look so beautiful.

She introduced me to her friend, a Dr. Hoffmann, with whom she was going to spend her afternoon off. As they made their way towards Kurfürstendamm, I was struck by the ease with which they walked side by side. I felt both envy and a new sense of loss. Someone had intruded and would take Fräulein Herta away from me. No doubt she was more interested in him than in me. Taking two steps at a time, I raced up the circular stairway to our apartment. Did my mother know about Fräulein Herta's friend?

"What's the hurry?" called meddlesome Frau Müller, as the elevator made its way to her third-floor apartment, right above ours. A short, quick woman with a quivering nose and a slight lisp, she was someone to be avoided at all costs. Anything more than polite cordiality on our part signaled to her a desire to be friends. Such an inadvertent gesture would result in an immediate invitation to her apartment for coffee where I would have to endure her gossip as well as her husband and two sons who towered over me like ungainly weather vanes and talked nonsense besides.

To my surprise, my mother was fully informed. Fräulein Herta had confided in her some time ago. She had met Dr. Hoffmann a year ago, on the train ride home from her summer vacation. "He wants to marry her and emigrate with her to America," said my mother, "But her parents refuse to let her go."

Now I understood the reason for the tension on weekends in Pankow and Fräulein Herta's atypical withdrawal and agitation. "What's she going to do? Will she marry him?"

"She can't decide, but it's my hunch that she will find it hard to leave her parents."

"But if she loves him, she should go with him," I uttered with adolescent fervor. "I certainly would!"

During the next few weeks, there was no sign of Dr. Hoffmann. I shadowed a taciturn and morose Fräulein Herta from room to room. She did not talk to me about her friend. Much to my amazement, a novel alliance had formed between my mother and her. Behind the closed doors of my mother's dressing room, I overheard an interminable hum of chatter, without being able to discern the actual words. A teary Fräulein Herta emerged. Clutching a soaked handkerchief, looking neither right nor left, she made her way back to her room.

While my romantic hopes and wishes for her new life in America never came to pass, I was grateful for her continued presence, even though the Nüremberg Laws would force her to leave me soon thereafter.

Watching Fräulein Herta pack, I tried to convince myself that now, at almost thirteen, I no longer needed such a companion. Certainly none of my classmates had a Kinderfräulein, and her presence set me apart from them even more.

As it turned out, I never had a chance to bid Fräulein Herta adieu. One afternoon, when I returned from school, she was no longer there to greet me. All her belongings were gone.

Someone else I loved had left. Even months after her departure, I went through my daily routine in a trance. There was nobody to fill the void. Her leaving had robbed me of

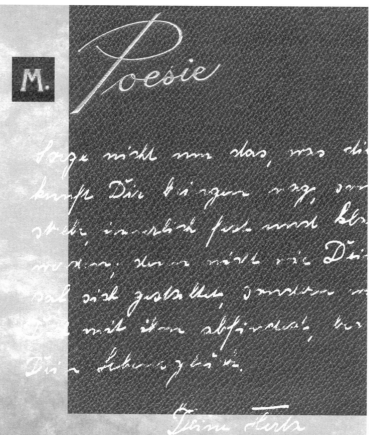

DON'T WORRY ABOUT WHAT THE FUTURE HOLDS FOR YOU,
BUT STRIVE TO BECOME SURE AND CLEAR WITHIN YOURSELF.
IT IS NOT WHAT FATE DEALS YOU,
BUT HOW YOU DEAL WITH IT
THAT WILL DETERMINE YOUR LIFE COURSE.

I WILL KEEP YOU IN LOVING REMEMBRANCE.

YOUR HERTA,
BERLIN, 1937

an island of safety and reliability. How would I survive?

No one in my family ever heard from her again. Yet her dependable presence and unconditional support left an indelible mark on me, the growing girl.

HANS, FRÄULEIN HERTA
AND MARIANNE

TANTE TONI AND MARIANNE 1930

CHAPTER 7
TANTE TONI

After Fräulein Herta's departure in spring of 1937, Tante Toni gained a new significance in my life. Until then, I mainly remember her TASSELED PILLOWS AND FLOWERS as sharing meals with us or as letting me

visit her in her room from time to time. Now that I was bereft of Fräulein Herta, my visits to her domain next to my brother's room became more frequent and assumed a greater urgency.

"Come in," beckoned my aunt's deep-throated voice as I knocked, seeking refuge from my unpredictable mother. "Don't take her so seriously," she said, calming my turbulent feelings, much as she had placated Fräulein Herta, Else or Anna, who were periodically offended by mother's fitful tactlessness. "She's probably not feeling well."

Looking back, I see my aunt's function in our household as that of a vigilant and benign spirit. She promoted harmony, earning her way by smoothing the effects of my mother's capriciousness. All this was indisputably done out of love and affection for her brother Julek, to whose well-being she was irrefutably committed.

Going into Tante Toni's room seemed like a trip to a distant realm, one of sunshine and warmth, far away from the somber and aseptic world that my mother had created at the other end of our strung-out apartment. With the exception of the somewhat brighter colors in her dressing room, my mother surrounded herself with colors of plain green, brown, and beige and with straight-edged massive oak furniture. My aunt's room teemed with color and comfort. Its casual disarray made me feel at home, although it never failed to elicit derogatory remarks from my mother.

"Doesn't she ever clean up her room?" she would complain to my father, who countered with a curt "What do you care?"

Books, clothing and newspapers were strewn on the floor and chairs. With the exception of the upright piano against the long wall, which had been in the room before Tante Toni's arrival, everything was drooping and round. Her curved couch, in flaming red and purple fabric, sagged in the middle and flattened the tassels against the oriental carpet.

My aunt loved tassels. Like cherries from a tree, they hung from the couch, the easy chair, the drapes, the keys of the wardrobe and the chest of drawers. Even the multicolored pillows had tasselled borders. Tante Toni waited for me to notice each new addition to her pillow collection, and then with glee would tell me of her discovery, first spotted in the window of an antique shop, and finally bought weeks later if the price was right. Anything too costly, she designed herself. I would find her hunched over, threading her red, blue or purple yarns for a new petit-point pillow.

"Does your mother know you're here?" she would ask protectively. With a "who cares" attitude, I settled down for a game of gin rummy or sixty-six. My mother abhorred card games. To her, they were a waste of time. She would watch disdainfully as Tante Toni left for her Wednesday afternoon card parties. My own interest in cards was equally denigrated. Often my vexed mother appeared at my aunt's door, determined to drag me away from this cozy paradise, and dispatch me to my room to polish up on French irregular verbs.

I found cards fascinating, and marveled at the tricks my aunt created, usually with an enriched repertoire after her weekly card parties. With Svengali-like concentration, she treated me to mysterious feats, greeting my perplexity with a grin that crinkled up her crab-apple cheeks. Ensconced in her plushy, oversized chairs, we were oblivious to noise and time passing, to the comings and goings of others in the household.

My aunt used to interrupt our card games long enough to core and quarter an apple without ever peeling the skin. "The best part of the apple is under the skin," she said. She firmly believed in the curative quality of apples and attributed her excellent health to this daily routine. A heavy crystal bowl, on a four-inch pedestal, remained a permanent fixture among the clutter on her chest of drawers. Light filtered through the cut glass, adding a luster to the green, red and yellow apples whose pungent aroma I still associate with her.

Tante Toni also initiated me into the mysteries of double solitaire. After watching her interminable games, I was invited to join her in what turned into strident battles, cards and palms pounding the coffee table, in a breathless race to be the first to get rid of our cards. Our immaculate scoring pads determined who dropped the pfennig in the kitty. The accrued amount was spent on an afternoon outing to a café on Kurfürstendamm, where we treated ourselves to pastries, hot chocolate, and coffee, and watched the world go by.

If my mother resented my attachment to Tante Toni, she never said so. Nonetheless, tell-tale signs of aggravation did surface occasionally. Deep sighs suggested exasperation with my aunt's ever-cheerful greeting upon my mother's return from her habitual outings. With a barely audible response, my mother escaped to the solitude of her dressing room, from where she would emerge, serene once more, in time for the noon meal.

Tante Toni moved in with us when I was eleven. Her husband, Kurt, had just died, and her son, Fritz, had emigrated to the United States, once the required affidavit from our gum-chewing Onkel Benno had arrived. Neither husband nor son had made spectacular successes of their lives, but Fritz's departure held great promise. In America, the land of unlimited possibilities, he would strike it rich and permit Tante Toni to follow shortly. Fritz's letters from New York became eagerly awaited events. They told about the skyscrapers, the Rockettes in Radio City, the Negroes playing jazz in Harlem night spots, and the millionaires in chauffeured limousines.

However, accounts of his work were sketchy at best. This absence of clarity permitted Tante Toni to indulge her fantasies. They made Fritz's allusions to a sweat shop a desirable and romantic place to work. "As soon as he saves enough money, he'll send for me," she repeated with a fervent optimism that diminished with the passing of time.

Tante Toni's life had been a series of disappointments which nonetheless did not leave her embittered. Much like my father, she tried to make the best of things and considered complaining useless, and like the knights and ladies in quest of the unicorn embroidered on her easy chairs, she was still searching for the silver lining. My father had repeatedly rescued Onkel Kurt from bankruptcy. Once, he promoted a joint business venture between Kurt and my Onkel Martin, by helping establish a quilting workshop. He purchased the necessary machinery, and paid for employee training. The partnership was of short duration. Onkel Kurt, the designated business manager, pocketed whatever meager

MARIANNE,
TANTE TONI,
ONKEL KURT
AND HANS,
1930

profits the young company realized, and squandered them on his two weaknesses, horses and women.

My father financed the re-organization of the business, with Onkel Martin at the helm. With tenacity and hard work from the entire family, Onkel Martin, Tante Rosel and my cousins Hannah and Steffi, the company became one of the most prestigious quilting ateliers in Berlin. Loyal clients continued to place clandestine orders even after the Nazis closed down the business.

Onkel Martin never spoke to Onkel Kurt again. Only after Onkel Kurt's syphilitic demise did Onkel Martin reestablish contact with his half-sister Toni. Vague rumors about my aunt's wish to divorce Onkel Kurt had floated about, but dissipated like clouds. Only the rich could afford such extravagance. She stuck with him to the end.

The fact that my cousin Fritz appeared to be as unsuccessful as his father was of no concern to me. He indulged me with his hilarious stories and his attention, and I in turn adored him. His dimpled face with its apple-red cheeks resembled his mother's and at Christmas, he transformed himself into the perfect Santa Claus.

Our family's celebration of Christmas was never questioned until the rise of Hitler. In my mother's Silesian family, it was a national holiday, devoid of religious connotations. While Christmas festivities would have been unthinkable in Pleschen, my enlightened father accepted it unhesitatingly. *Man muss die Feste feiern wie sie kommen*, (joyful occasions need to be celebrated as they occur), he would say with twinkling eyes.

And Christmas in Berlin was a magical time — extravagantly beautiful window displays in all the stores up and down Kurfürsterdenen — festive displays in the toy departments of all the major department stores — and then the *Weihnechtsmarkt* — The Christmas Fair — *Unter den Linden.* Decorated merchant booths — one after another —

offered a tantalizing assortment of roasted chestnuts, candy and toys. Small groups of organ grinders and Christmas carolers filled the streets with joyous sights and sounds. People of all ages bundled up in colorful scarves and hats, seemingly oblivious to the cold and snow. Amid twinkling street lights and vapor trails of steamy breath, vendors briskly rubbed their gloved hands and beckoned us to buy from their festive displays. Having been given a little money, I was delighted to spend it!

Christmas was also a tribute to Fräulein Herta, Else, and Anna, who spent Christmas Eve with us before leaving the following morning to be with their families.

For once, the somber, dimly lit *Herrenzimmer* came alive with a small tree which we decorated with the help of Fräulein Herta and even my mother. Down from the attic came boxes of collected ornaments. Soon the tree sparkled with balls of silver, blue, and red. Silver streamers were thrown over the branches, carved wooden apples and toys were intermingled with multi-colored candy ornaments, and small metal holders with white candles were snapped in place.

Our task completed, we were sent to our rooms, where we anxiously awaited the arrival of Santa Claus. A heavily disguised Fritz, in a Santa outfit, and with a bulky sack by his side, was miraculously seated in a chair near the tree. With jokes and reprimands, he knowingly reminded us of our most recent misdeeds. His benign forgiveness was punctuated by presenting gaily wrapped gifts that he slowly extracted from a big gunnysack, with repeated admonitions to us to continue to be good and studious children in the year to come.

A beaming entourage of adults, including Fräulein Herta and Else, watched this annual spectacle with undiluted joy. They happily accompanied us in vigorous singing of *Oh Tannenbaum, Ruhe Nacht Heilige Nacht, Es ist ein Ros' entsprungen* and *Alle Jahre wieder kommt das Christus Kind.*

Christmas presents for my brother and for me consisted of modest items — a toy, a book — or a needed item of clothing. We could always count on a paper plate, imprinted with delicate green fir branches, filled to the brim with marzipan potatoes, marzipan-filled chocolate wreaths, anise cookies, Pfeffernüsse, tangerines, nuts, and raisins. Else or Fräulein Herta walked away with more substantial gifts. Their beautifully wrapped packages contained nightgowns, blouses, sweaters, soap, cologne and a generous check.

Else opened the french doors to the dining room. Amid flickering candlelight, and the pungent scent of the fir tree, we partook of a traditional Christmas Eve dinner of sweet-and-sour carp in a brown raisin sauce and potato dumplings. Warned not to polish off the entire contents of our Christmas plate, my brother and I were finally sent to bed. The adults finished the evening with hot spiced wine and brandy.

The last time that Christmas festivities took place at Brandenburgische Strasse was in 1934. It was the last time that my great buddies Rolf and Ludwig, the grandchildren of my father's half-sister Rosa, and Gerhart and Eveline, Onkel Herman's children from Görlitz, raced through the corridors of our vast apartment in a wild game of hide-and-go-seek; the last time that we all ate Dresden and poppy-seed stollen together; and, donning galoshes and winter coats, sloshed through the snow of *Preussen Park* to build a snowman of monumental proportions.

By the following year, Fritz had departed for New York, Onkel Herman and his family had begun their trek to Oregon, and Rolf and Ludwig's father, forced to resign his teaching post in Stettin, no longer could afford visits to Berlin. Like many potential emigrés, Arthur and his wife explored new career possibilities. He took up accounting. Herta, Tante Rosa's daughter, became apprenticed to a confectioner. Other friends of my parents became adept in carpentry, bookbinding, plumbing, distilling liqueurs — new skills that could provide them with a livelihood in the future.

When Tante Toni reflected on an occupation for her new life in America, (after all, she didn't want to be a burden to her son), she talked about working in a flower shop. Her green thumb made all flowers flourish. A wide bay window in her room that extended onto Ravensberger Strasse contained an array of plants that thrived under her care. My interest in plants was nil, and, while I was unaware of the vigilance that went into their maintenance, I loved this little corner, with its flowering cacti, broad-leafed rubber plants, lacy ferns and dainty African violets. Some of the plants rested in white porcelain Meissen containers; others sat humbly in common red clay pots.

The upright piano in her room required my aunt's tolerance of my daily practicing. At one time, my mother had harbored hopes that I would have a voice worth developing, while my father equally wished that I would emulate his favorite and talented cousin, Greta, who was a fine pianist. An embarrassed silence followed my coerced playing of Chopin's *Valse Triste* during one of Greta's visits from Chemnitz. She was obviously pained at having to listen to my musical attempts, but it was I who was irretrievably shamed. Besides wanting to impress her, I had a mad crush on her handsome son Walter, and had hoped that my musical talent would make him aware of my existence. Confronted by my utter failure in eliciting even his most fleeting interest, and furious at my father for having placed me in this humiliating situation, I escaped to my yellow-walled sanctuary from where I did not emerge until long after Greta's departure.

My own attitude toward the piano was a mixture of boredom, anxiety and frustration on one hand, and delight and exhilaration on the other. I was thrilled to get a Mozart Fantasy or a Beethoven Sonata right. Tante Toni, who admired anything I played, no matter how badly, was an uncritical and reassuring audience. Yet never for a moment did I fool myself into thinking that I had talent.

Frau Margraf, my patient and always encouraging piano teacher, was solely responsible for even the smallest of my musical successes. She may have sensed that, beyond music, she could promote in me a general loosening up. Much to my surprise, she even seemed to genuinely like me, notwithstanding my moodiness and undistinguished musical accomplishments. She showed interest in my thoughts — a vast departure from my family, who either did not listen to me or made fun of my occasional flights of fancy. The fact that I preferred music in the minor key piqued her curiosity. Here was someone who actually took me seriously!

At the outset, Frau Margraf came to our apartment for my weekly lessons. Later, either with Fräulein Herta or alone, I walked to her apartment on Hohenzollern Damm, a cheerful flat, filled with light, low-slung furniture and modern art. It reflected the lightheartedness and joy that I associated with her. She and her young lawyer husband were still in the process of furnishing the flat. What sort of man did such a special individual marry? I wondered.

Frau Margraf's warmth and energy made me feel more optimistic about myself. To be like her some day was my ardent hope. She had a trim and sporty look, a round face framed by short cropped dark hair, wore fashionable clothes, and impressed me with her ease and general rightness. In contrast to my mother's awkwardness in expressing herself, Frau Margraf's ability to put thoughts and feelings into words was a revelation.

What utter disappointment to finally meet her husband. I had imagined a tall and cheerful man. I thought he would be like my favorite partner from dancing class with whom I stumbled through the foxtrot, tango and lambeth walk and whose tantalizingly fragrant hair pomade, drifting down from his Olympian heights, set my heart aflutter.

Instead, Frank was chubby and short. His curly reddish-brown hair was his nicest feature. A condescending and unfriendly manner made me feel like an intruder. Whatever did she see in him? Relations between men and women were full of mystery.

Early in 1937, Frau Margraf invited me for tea to break the news that she and her husband were leaving for Holland. "A young Jewish lawyer had no future in Nazi Germany," she said. I sat on her packing cases, in tears, inconsolable. Another person important to me was leaving me behind.

She must have anticipated my sadness, as she had in readiness a delicate jewelry box in dark blue velvet, containing a gold charm in the form of a small piano. We promised to write to each other. Before making our farewells, I asked her to write in my *Poesie Album*, a six-inch-square book bound in textured brown leather, initialed in gold, with many of its pages already filled with proverbs, poems, and personal remembrances from friends, classmates, and teachers. Her entry resounds qualities of her cheerfulness: *Mit Instrument und Flötenspiel vertreibt man Sorg und Unmut viel*. (With instrument and flute playing, we drive away worry and discontent.)

Although her departure signaled the end of my official piano studies, it was not the end of my love of music. I would go to the piano, often during Tante Toni's absence so as not to disturb her with my faulty playing, and practice the Chopin waltzes, Beethoven Sonatas and Mozart Fantasies that I had memorized with Frau Margraf.

It never seemed to occur to my parents to take me to concerts, but luckily Tante Toni filled that void. Together we listened to opera on the radio, especially when her idol, Richard Tauber, was singing. When Jews were no longer permitted to attend performances in the Berlin Concert Halls, she invited me to accompany her to concerts and operas presented by the *Jüdischen Kultur Bund*, an organization administered by the city's Jewish community. It was strangely comforting to be surrounded by an entirely Jewish audience. While the modest performance hall could not be compared to the splendor of either the Berliner Staatsoper or the Komische Oper, the performances were of such high artistic quality that many non-Jews asked to be illegally smuggled in, at their own risk.

Founded in 1933 to create an outlet for Jewish performers and directors who were being forced out of German cultural life, the *Kultur Bund* kept alive the European intellectual tradition which was being squelched by the Nazis. There, the music of Mahler, Schoenberg and Tchaikowsky could be heard; there, the plays of non-Germans such as Shakespeare, Molière, Molnar and Pirandello were presented.

Tante Toni and I were grateful beneficiaries of this lifeline. Thanks to her, I was introduced to *A Masked Ball*, *The Barber of Seville*, and *Madame Butterfly*. My friend Reni, whose non-Jewish uncle continued to take her to the Staatsoper, listened rather condescendingly to accounts of my operatic outings in these less than luxurious settings as, on our endless walks through Berlin, we regaled Elisabeth with the operas' dramatic plots.

But I forgave Reni her disdain. I understood! I knew the difference. I too had been irretrievably seduced by the glorious splendor of the Berliner Staatsoper. It was at Christmastime; I was eight years old. Dressed in one of Frau Kralert's smocked creations of navy-blue velvet, I nestled in the softness of my red plush orchestra seat, my eyes glued to the magic of Rumpelstilschen unfolding on the stage. Costumes, masks, music, sets, and the silence of an attentive audience, all had me transfixed. It's profound impact stayed with me forever.

While my aunt tried valiantly to keep up a cheerful facade, daily events were beginning to erode that gaiety. Her card-playing circle was disbanding, its members leaving for distant lands. Bravely finding excuses for the lack of letters from Fritz, she became more inward and, for me, less available. Although she did not openly complain, she found ways to fill the void. While a weekly trip to the library had sufficed in the past, she now set off Tuesdays and Fridays and returned laden with a supply of romances and adventure stories in which she lost herself amongst her pillows and tassels.

"There she goes," my mother would remark with disdain, "getting more of those *Schmoekers*," (low-brow romances). She also referred to such books as *Hintertreppen Romane*, backstairs romances, which conjured up illicit and perilous encounters of maids, washer women, prostitutes and truck drivers on poorly lit and clammy back stairs of otherwise luxury dwellings.

Needless to say, no such books lined the carved mahogany bookshelves in our *Herrenzimmer*. Goethe, Schiller, Fichte, Heine, and Shakespeare, leather-bound and gold-leafed, stood along the corner wall. Thomas Mann, Galsworthy, Upton Sinclair and Gerhart Hauptman were added over the years. I often wondered whether the books were read or whether, like our dull oil paintings of still lives and pastoral scenes, they merely decorated the wall.

But Tante Toni's books were read. Just as Frau Margraf reminded me to make music when troubled, I realized how Tante Toni's library enriched her life and distracted her from her worries. Sitting next to my aunt on the droopy couch, eating sliced applies and sucking rock candy, I listened as she recounted stories of loneliness, surprise encounters, love, jealousy and resignation. She was an imaginative and vivid story-teller and no doubt occasionally embellished on the real text. Her style followed such a predictable pattern of

WITH INSTRUMENT AND FLUTE PLAYING,
WE DRIVE AWAY WORRY AND DISCONTENT.

FRAU MARGRAF
DECEMBER, 1935

beginning, middle and end that I soon anticipated the outcome of her stories. I loved happy endings, and was elated when noble but downtrodden characters won out.

My love for books did not spring from any abundance in the nursery. As a very young child, I remember mainly *Strubelpeter*, a picture book, that had become a staple in

4ᵀᴴ BIRTHDAY CELEBRATION FOR HANS (FOREGROUND), WITH MARIANNE AND PETER, 1931.

BIRTHDAY GIFTS AND   CHOCOLATE BUNDT CAKE
SWEDISH CANDLEHOLDER   TOY TRACTOR AND TOY FIRE ENGINE

German households. I loved and dreaded this anything-but-innocent book with its huge threatening scissors that cut mercilessly away at bushy hair or over-sized, elongated fingernails, and evoked fear of dire punishment for any misdeed. By contrast, *Hopsie das Kaninchen* (Hopsie the Rabbit) was a charming and benign book with beautiful pastel illustrations which was brought by the Easter Bunny when, at aged six, I was in bed with flu. *Hopsie,* the best friend of two children who were the same age as my brother and myself, unfailingly allied himself with them against the injustices and intrusions of the outside world.

A few years later, Erich Kästner became my hero. I knew his books almost by heart: *Emil and the Detectives*, *Pünktchen and Anton* and *Das Fliegende Klassenzimmer* (The Flying Classroom). Here was someone who understood me and my growing pains. Emil Fishbein, Anton Gast and Pony Hütchen became unforgettable characters I admired for their intelligence, sense of adventure, generosity and goodness. Devoid of sentimentality, these larger-than-life characters stood up to the hypocrisy and vanity of parents and adults in general.

Two more enchanting companions on my Görlitz bedside table were the stories of the Brothers Grimm and those of Hans Christian Anderson. The latter, in gold-embossed pigskin, had been my father's engagement present to my mother in September, 1921. I loved the illustrations in both, but always preferred the gruesome, bold drawing in Grimm to the delicate, restrained watercolors in Anderson.

Despite the occasional tensions of everyday life, I never doubted the unwavering devotion and loyalty my parents and Tante Toni felt toward each other. They would often chat together until late at night in the *Herrenzimmer* or in my aunt's room. Increasingly they gathered in Tante Toni's room behind locked doors. My knocking to gain the accustomed admission received a curt admonition to go back to bed. Soon, someone would come to kiss me good-night.

These mysterious sessions took place during the early part of 1938. No matter what questions I posed to satisfy my curiosity, no clarification was forthcoming. Blank faces stared back at me. Once, when I unexpectedly burst into my aunt's room after school, I noticed that she was involved in an unusual activity. Spools of thread, needles, scissors and cloth-covered buttons lay scattered all around her. Her colorful pillows were buried under piles of dresses, jackets and coats. In the midst of this immense disorder sat my aunt, serenely replacing the buttons on all these garments. "They are prettier," she said. "Fritz wrote about the new fashion in the States."

It was not until much later, when we were safely out of Germany, that my parents revealed the truth. During those evenings, and deep into the night, the three of them were operating a button-making machine. My aunt placed a metal back onto the machine; my father jammed a minutely folded money bill onto the metal ring; and my mother covered it with a piece of cloth. The impact of the hand-operated lever of the machine produced a button that was sewn onto our clothing.

With this chancy stratagem, my parents attempted to take with them to America what was rightfully theirs. The Nazi government had placed strict limits on the amount of money that could be taken out of Germany. They confiscated the private property of emigrating Jews with impunity. In an attempt to circumvent this measure, many of our friends acquired valuable objects like cameras, paintings, books and jewelry, intending to turn them into cash upon reaching their destination. My parents had purchased a number of Leica cameras, which at that time were in high demand in America. I'm grateful that they had kept me unaware of these hazardous maneuvers.

When moving day finally came in September, 1938, our innocent looking clothes with their multitude of buttons were carefully packed into boxes and suitcases. They were placed in a big moving van along with the small antiques, acquired with the help of the Baroness, replacing our bulky Prussian furniture that had outgrown its usefulness. In the States, one had small pieces of furniture, and we wanted to fit in. Those valuable garments were further accompanied by all the household essentials, my new Torpedo portable typewriter, garments for every possible occasion, linens for my future dowry, and my father's 1938 Buick. After a nod of approval from the customs official (Did a few hundred marks change hands?) this non-descript container whose full significance would be lost on anyone but us, began its journey down Brandenburgische Strasse. Our possessions would travel across the Atlantic, through the Panama Canal, and northward up the Pacific Ocean to Oregon, where we would eventually claim them and unpack them in our as yet unknown new home.

The entire operation of vacating the apartment had left me numb. Hollow footsteps echoed from the now uncarpeted hardwood floors. The movers boisterously maneuvered packing cases on ropes down the large windows of the *Herrenzimmer* or over the balcony of my parents' bedroom. These sounds reverberated through an apartment I no longer knew. I moved in a daze. What would become of us all?

SUNDAY OUTING IN JULIAN'S NEW CAR. JULIAN IS ON THE HOOD; HANS, MARIANNE AND LUTZ MOOS ARE ON TOP.

COSTUME PARTY AT CAMP WOLFSHAU,
SUMMER 1938

With the inexorable tight-ening of the Nazi net, and growing overt anti-Sem-itism, an increasing number of Jewish parents enrolled their children in Jewish schools. In Berlin, they could choose

HOHENZOLLERN
LYZEUM CIRCA
1934

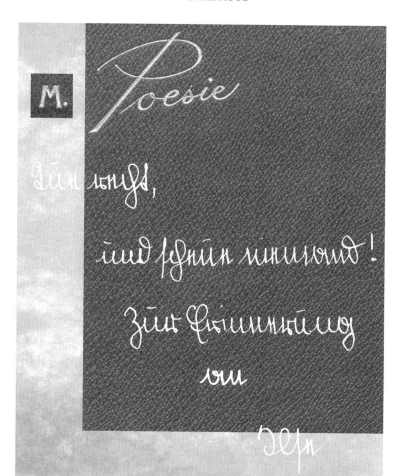

ACT JUSTLY,
AND FEAR NO ONE!

IN REMEMBRANCE OF

ILSE
SEPTEMBER 26, 1935

between a number of excellent institutions, including the Goldschmidt, Lessler, or Kaliski schools, all of which rapidly filled up. Some of my Jewish classmates from the Meyer School, such as Steffi Friedman, Eva Klopstock and Dorchen Oppenheim, were enrolled in the Lessler Schule.

My brother was transferred to the Goldschmidt school in his second year of grade school. Public school teachers, either convinced of the validity of Nazi ideology or afraid of the consequences dare they not follow prescribed attitudes were now given license to torment and ridicule Jewish children and at times accuse them of offenses of which they were innocent. In the first grade, my brother was accused of stealing money from a gentile classmate. Even though the real culprit was eventually discovered, my brother was never exonerated.

Although the Hohenzollern Lyzeum was not devoid of anti-Semitism, it was on the whole unusually tolerant of its Jewish students, especially in 1934, in the first year of high school. Not one of my classmates refrained from signing my Poesie Album. There were fewer entries after 1935. Our class room teachers (Ilse Oheim, Hilde Leicht, Dr. Ericksen, and my very favorite, Fräulein Müller) actually went out of their way to make the Jewish students feel welcome and included. Only the music teacher treated us as if we were undesirable citizens. To him, we were invisible. He excluded us from recitals, denigrated us by making racist jokes and, when addressing us, did so with undisguised contempt.

Essentially timid and unsure of myself, I did not expect much from my surroundings and took it rather for granted that I would not be included in after-school activities or visits to the homes of my classmates. Nonetheless, I could not help wonder why the girls, who were not so different from me, were reluctant to be friends. Certainly they were not born anti-Semitic. Perhaps their parents encouraged them to keep their distance. It might have been the influence of the BDM,

Bund Deutscher Mädchen, the Nazi organization for young girls. Not everyone in my class belonged, but those who did came to school in their uniforms of navy skirts, white blouses and red kerchiefs imprinted with the swastika. At times they greeted one another with the Nazi salute of *Heil Hitler*, their right arms extended upward.

This strained atmosphere notwithstanding, I did not experience my years at Hohenzollern Lyzeum as excessively traumatic or painful. I looked forward to each new day at school, enjoyed learning and being in a group, even though I was generally on the periphery. There was comfort in my close relationships with Reni and Elisabeth, and in the more casual ones with Helga Blumenthal, Ilse Blum, Ursula Pinkus and Helga Hoerniss. The fact that some of these girls were only half Jewish made very little difference. They were equally shunned.

Yet there were a few exceptions. There was Liselotte, my ski buddy, who seemed not to care that I was Jewish, and Anita Knöedel, in whose company I always felt accepted

LYZEUM CLASS
CIRCA 1937

and protected. And then there was Gisela. She and I smoked cigarettes in our Schrebergarten, experimented with makeup, and openly made fun of Hitler. I knew nothing about her parents, yet she impressed me enormously with her refreshing candor.

During my last year in Berlin, my parents sent my brother and me to a Jewish summer camp in Wolfshau in the *Riesengebirge*. This all-Jewish setting differed from the Lyzeum where I was always on guard. At the Camp, I had an unfamiliar sense of safety and comfort that permitted me to be myself. Common interest and taste, not religion, determined the basis for friendship.

Even though this 1938 mountain vacation gave us many opportunities to enjoy a summer with a wide range of diverse activities, a heavy cloud hung over us. Everybody was talking about their families' plans to leave. *Die Auswanderung,* the emigration, and uncertainty of the future was manifested by sleeplessness in the younger children, and irritability in the older ones.

I dealt with the tension by actively seeking new friends. Ruth, a tall, athletic girl, had arrived at Camp with a younger brother who trailed us constantly and interrupted our conversation. He short-sheeted us, put frogs in our beds, spied on us when we undressed and laughed at our unsuccessful attempts to catch him. To escape him, we went off on long hikes where he could not follow, and sealed a friendship we expected to last forever.

Ruth's parents spent the summer packing for their move to England. Others at camp talked of emigrating to North or South America, Australia, or Palestine. There were also those who had no plans at all.

The two other girls in our cabin were Irma and Trude, who Ruth and I considered flighty and silly. They had no interest in books. Their hair was permed, they wore nail polish, and took off in the woods to meet the older boys. We

USCHI STEIN (CENTER) WITH FELLOW CAMPERS AT
SUMMER CAMP IN WOLFSHAU IN THE RIESENGEBIRGE, 1938

had nothing in common with them.

In the adjoining cabin were three girls from Düsseldorf, Sara, Steffi and Gaby. They asked me along on their hikes, had me sit next to them at meals, and (much to Ruth's annoyance) invited me to their cabin. For some reason, they had picked me as a possible convert to Zionism, a cause they passionately espoused. They talked about the excitement of founding a homeland where Jews would live in peace and harmony. They were learning modern Hebrew, sang Zionist songs, taught me to dance the Horah, and urged me to join a Zionist youth group once I returned to Berlin. Their enthusiasm was hard to resist. They handed me essays by Theodore Herzl, pamphlets on the first Zionist Congress in Switzerland in 1897, and on Zionist thought. I learned about life on the kibbutz, and came to realize that communal life could be thrilling and useful at the same time.

Ruth was outraged. "A Jewish State will never solve the Jewish problem," she lectured me. "The land is infertile, the Arabs are lazy and they detest the Jews. Go ahead, be a Zionist, but you and I won't be friends any longer." Her sudden outbursts reminded me of those of my mother and made me wonder about our friendship. I had begun to like the girls from Düsseldorf. I admired their commitment to an ideal, and regretted my ignorance. Zionism was not a household word at home. My parents donated small amounts of money to Zionist causes, but had never

HANS, SECOND FROM LEFT, WITH FELLOW CAMPERS AT WOLFSHAU IN THE RIESENGEBIRGE, 1938

contemplated emigrating to Palestine. The only active Zionist I knew was Ati, the daughter of my mother's childhood friend, Hilde. Ati's concerns at the end of the 1930's were a far cry from those of our mothers, who, two decades earlier, embroidered handkerchiefs and walked their dogs through the Silesian countryside. But Ati never shared her Zionist zeal with me. No doubt she considered me unenlightened and unsuited for the life of a pioneer. She was probably right.

One night toward the end of summer, my three Düsseldorf friends invited me to share with them cookies sent from home. They also needed to tell me something about my estranged friend, Ruth.

"First of all," began Sara, whose short curly black hair bobbed up and down with every word, "Ruth no longer likes you. She thinks you are a Polish Jew because of your name, Schybilski. She also claims that only Polish Jews go to Palestine. She acts superior because her family has lived here in Germany over 200 years. No doubt her parents will return from England the moment Hitler is gone."

Sara's mention of Polish Jews reminded me of my own family's prejudice which, much to my dismay, was shared by a great number of German Jews. "Give them some money and send them on," was a familiar refrain. The presence of Polish Jews provoked discomfort and embarrassment. With their faulty German, their strange-sounding Yiddish, and their orthodoxy, they could jeopardize the status of the German Jew, which, as we began to realize, hung in a precarious balance any way.

"Ruth and her parents are ostriches," added Steffi, the most serious of the three. She was the daughter of a Düsseldorf rabbi whose pride in his Jewishness and impassioned commitment to Zionism had rubbed off on his daughter.

"Anti-Semitism has always existed, everywhere. My father says that by founding our own state, the world will begin to respect us, and recognize us for who we really are."

I was impressed by her fervor and authority, and I was intrigued when she asked whether I had ever heard of Vladimir Jabotinsky. Of course I hadn't. Steffi described him as a radical thinker who was her parents' mentor. He disagreed with Herzl's gradual approach to the founding of a Jewish state and wanted the immediate end of English rule.

Gaby chimed in. "Our parents are different from the followers of Herzl, and certainly from uncommitted people like Ruth and her parents, who consider themselves superior."

Did I blush? I certainly fit that mold. Where had I been all these years? Had the Hohenzollern Lyzeum and even my parents' indifference isolated me from the true concern of being Jewish? Though I could not think of anything significant to add, I wanted to set one thing straight.

"You're wrong about only Polish Jews emigrating to Palestine. My friend Ati will soon go there, and she has the complete support of her parents. Her family has lived in Germany for centuries. Her father is a highly respected judge in Berlin, was an officer during the last war, and, like my father, was awarded the Iron Cross for bravery."

I thought I had made my point, but the discussion continued. What about her parents? Where will they go?

If they had known Hilde Kamm's family, they would not have asked. In no way could I imagine the judge and his wife, the gentle, saintly Tante Hilde, dig potatoes or share a primitive cottage with other families. In addition, Ati's frail and lovely grandmother, and close friend of my Grandmother Lina and to whom I paid my yearly visit during Rosh Hashana services at the Fasanen Strasse Synagogue, was no candidate for a rugged pioneer life on a Kibbutz.

"To go to Palestine seems wonderful," I added. "But it's

not for everyone. My parents wouldn't fit in. My mother is so spoiled, she doesn't even do her own cooking."

The three looked at each other. "You've got a point," said Gaby. "My mother said that people who don't fit would be a burden."

The indomitable Steffi would not give up. "All that may be true, but we need a homeland, where everyone is welcome."

I could not have agreed more. But I knew that once I was again home, my parents would jeer at my ardor. Furthermore, we were headed for America, where life seemed less rigorous, less demanding.

Letters from my cousin Eveline from Oregon confirmed this. She wrote about her co-ed junior high school, about a boyfriend who took her on dates to a drugstore for milk shakes, cokes and hamburgers. What were all these unfamiliar things? She did her homework during study periods which left evenings free for going to movies or visiting friends. The lure of life on a Kibbutz paled in comparison.

From time to time, my brother came for a short visit to my adult cottage. He was homesick, and for once seemed glad to confide in me. Although he now attended a Jewish grade school, he was oblivious to the serious problems we were beginning to face. We felt the impact even at this peaceful mountain hamlet.

"Why does Hitler hate the Jews so?" he asked, in confused desperation. "They are nice. Everyone here is nice. They don't steal like Bruno and Max at my old school."

There was no way I could explain Hitler's obsession with a pure, super race, an Aryan state.

"Some things just can't be explained," I told him. "But because Hitler is so scary, we'll soon be leaving Germany. We're lucky to get out."

The days of Camp turned into weeks, then a month, and

HANS AND
MARIANNE
1938

when the end of the six-week period arrived, we were no longer Zionists, conservatives, Polish Jews, young children or venerable older ones. We accepted each other for what we were. Ruth and I had made up, and walked once more, arm in arm, along the mountain paths. I looked with admiration on my three Düsseldorf friends, whose idealism became a beacon in my life. We promised to write to one another, no matter where we would be.

"What a boon to our stamp collection!" jested Gaby, our habitual joker. Yet no one was particularly happy to leave. I clutched my brother, who no longer seemed to annoy me. Indeed, I was becoming increasingly fond of him, even protective. We climbed into the third-class railway carriage and returned to Berlin.

In the brilliant warm days of September and early October, the thermometer outside my yellow room registered seventy or eighty degrees, even in the morning. Dry leaves began to fall from the acacia tree. The way the sun reflected on the villa across the street told me fair weather would continue all week. The warm days kept us in summer clothes, which by now had become too short and too tight. My new fall outfits for school lay neglected at the bottom of the white Görlitz armoire.

Since the school year always began in Spring, no surprises lay in store for us as we resumed classes. With the exception of Elisabeth, and Flora Schaffai, the shy but friendly daughter of the Persian Ambassador to Berlin who joined our class in the second year, all twenty-two of us who had started in the Sexta were still together in the fall of 1938.

We settled into the routine of school, inspecting our books, inaugurating notebooks, sharpening pencils, perhaps even displaying real fountain pens. And, once again, the time for the Jewish High Holidays arrived.

I experienced this annual occurrence as a mixed blessing, an inconvenience, but also a thrill. I was reluctant to miss

HANS AND
MARIANNE 1937

school and felt uncomfortable about so obviously being different. Yet I revelled in the prospect of going to synagogue, listening to the prayers, hearing the familiar chanting of the cantor, and being sent by my mother to pay visits to her friends in our upstairs balcony for women. I became religious all over again and promised myself to attend services during the year, to learn Hebrew, to turn into a good Jew.

For my family, the High Holidays always brought the fact that we were Jews into renewed focus. While the ordinary bustle of life continued, for a few days the Jewish community became a world unto itself. Stores closed, students stayed home from school, families were reunited. An other-worldly calm descended on us. The streets smelled different and appeared distant, as if seen through a gossamer net. The general public, scurrying to and fro, seemed unaware of our profound mission. My fleeting religious inspirations filled me with a sense of superiority, and I considered all non-Jews heathens.

As in every previous year, Jews all over Berlin set out in somber clothes for the synagogue at sundown on the eve of Rosh Hashanah. The Orthodox traveled on foot; the Conservative, including us, by streetcar. Some men carried hat boxes containing their silk top hats they preferred to wear during the service rather than their everyday hats or yarmulkes. My father carried his gray hatbox, which also contained his talis, the white-and-black prayer shawl handed down from his father, Isaac.

After a three-block walk down Brandenburgische Strasse, we caught the streetcar that dropped us off near the synagogue on Fasanen Strasse. We filed in and from the women's balcony my mother and I scanned the male congregation until we spotted my father, unfamiliar in top hat and talis. His acknowledgment of us, though distant, left us content. We settled down for the service, alternately rising and sitting, watching the opening and closing of the

Torah, joined in the chanting and reading, and tried to pay attention to the sermon. That last year, I was mesmerized by the sermon of Joachim Prince, a dynamic visiting rabbi, who summoned us back to our Jewishness, urging us to take pride in the religion of our forefathers and to give wholehearted support to the cause of Zionism.

I could tell in advance my parents' reaction to the service. They always criticized the sermon, debated the quality of the cantor's chanting of the Kol Nidre prayer, gossiped about friends and poked fun at the women who appeared, even in the warmest of weather, in fur coats. Yet, staying away would have been unthinkable.

After the morning service of Yom Kippur, we went home briefly so that my parents could rest to alleviate the pangs of fasting. I usually did not return with them for the Memorial and Nile services, but waited impatiently at home for the breaking of the fast. This invariably started out with a shot of schnapps, marinated herring in sour cream with thinly sliced onions, a freshly baked Challah with butter and jam, and coffee. Dinner followed later, concluding the annual return to our cultural and religious roots.

There were times when I regretted my family's lack of interest in a more exacting observance of Jewish festivals. We never lit Friday-night Sabbath candles, we never attended religious services except for the High Holidays, and we celebrated Passover seriously, with all the required ritual, only when invited by Käte and Mo Eiseman, the Orthodox daughter and son-in-law of Tante Rosa.

On those occasions, again at sundown, we climbed up the four flights of stairs to the Eiseman apartment on Mommsen Strasse. On *Yontov* ("holiday" in Hebrew), Orthodox Jews do not use elevators or, for that matter, any form of motorized transportation. Turning on stoves, using vacuum cleaners, and ringing door bells were equally prohibited.

Käte and Mo always hired an assistant for Passover, the Shabat goy, who presided in a kitchen that had undergone a prolonged and meticulous cleaning. The everyday dishes, those for meat or for fish, had been stored and replaced with uncontaminated Passover dishes which now sparkled in the cupboard on freshly lined shelves. The entire house was Passover clean.

Cousin Mo, the customary leader of the Passover service, was a pale, nondescript man, with a dry and sardonic sense of humor. But his humor was not apparent at his reading of the *Haggadah*, the annual retelling of how the children of Israel were being led out of Egyptian bondage into the Promised Land. I was bored to distraction. Not understanding a word of Hebrew, I was scared of making a mistake when, sometimes, as the youngest, I was called on to ask the Four Questions, which I had tried to memorize. Except for my father, who occasionally winked at me, everyone was deadly serious and unsmiling. I found the Orthodoxy stifling and the food abominable. Even the matzoth balls tasted like a bland rubbery substance. They could not compare with my mother's delectable mouthfuls which, from an old Silesian family recipe required chopped nuts, sugar and soaked matzoth and which, with a strong broth of beef and chicken, made our less formalistic Passover with a *Haggadah* reading of never more than twenty minutes, memorable events.

"Nothing has changed since last year," my father would say. "Anna, bring in the soup!"

It was not that I was deprived of religious education. The Hohenzollen Lyzerum excused us Jewish girls from class when Protestant or Catholic religion was taught. By special arrangements, a Frau Hirsch arrived twice a month to instruct us in the Old Testament, basic Hebrew and the significance of the Jewish Holidays. She was an unfortunate choice, as dull and unimaginative as Mo Eiseman's Passover

Service. She kindled no spark of curiosity or excitement about Judaism. Her genuine kindness did not make up for her ineptness as a teacher. We began to find reason to be absent and, ultimately, Frau Hirsch was withdrawn. Our relief was intermingled with feelings of guilt since our capricious indifference had deprived her of this additional income.

Marianne and Reni 1938

CHAPTER 9
GOOD-BYE

BERLIN,
FALL 1938

A penetrating wind blew the leaves off the sidewalk as my mother and I walked toward our leased garden plot, near Preussen Park, to bid farewell to Reni and Elisabeth, my

MARIANNE (TOP) CELEBRATES HER 14TH BIRTHDAY WITH HER TWO CLOSEST FRIENDS, ELISABETH (LEFT) AND RENI (RIGHT), APRIL 1938

two closest friends. At four o'clock, on this grim Saturday afternoon following *Kristallnacht*, it was already turning dark, and lights were appearing in stores and windows along Brandenburgische Strasse. Yellow and brown leaves of poplar and oak trees, brittle and dry, lay curled along the pavements.

The sound of those leaves crunching beneath my step momentarily altered my sense of time and place — memories of carefree and happy times flashed through my mind — Sunday morning walks with my father in the Grunewald, unhurried strolls with Elisabeth and Reni along Ku-Damm and routine walks with Fräulein Herta to Preussen Park, to school or to Major Böhmer's gymnastic classes.

The Berlin seasons were defined for me by my clothing.

In spring, a candy-striped dress with matching socks and red sweater would replace the winter outfits in my closet. Berlin springs were unpredictable. Some years, the cherry trees would not burst into bloom until late May, but once it turned warm, I couldn't wait to leave my sweaters at home.

Under the thick carpet of leaves, I felt the large cement slabs whose dividing lines used to serve as the perimeters for my private games of hopscotch, as I skipped, hopped, or bounced, legs together or apart, never touching the lines, on the way to the Schrebergarten five minutes from our apartment. In summer, I would hop along these pavements of our neighborhood, in sleeveless cotton dresses with matching underpants and drawstring bags, or in my favorite red-and-white polka-dotted bib overalls. Pleated plaid skirts, navy-blue sweaters and white blouses with Peter Pan collars were my favorite fall outfits. The sweater I fought as long as I could. My full skirts billowed up in the air as I negotiated my jumps and hops, indifferent to the passers-by.

But today there was no jumping or hopping. It even felt wrong for me to admire my new peacock-blue coat in the reflection of a shop window. The coat's shapely lines made me feel grown-up and elegant. This was no moment for frivolous thoughts. My mother and I, in step, walked deep in thought. Her silence added to my discomfort. For once, I would have wished her less shy and restrained. But I needed her with me now, to bolster me for my farewells to Reni and Elisabeth. I needed her to protect me from feelings of guilt that we were able to leave while they had to stay on. How would I tell Reni and Elisabeth that we were leaving the next day?

Like goldfish in a bowl, the three of us were a unit, but changing formations constantly. Who would walk in the middle? Who spent more time with whom after school? Who was loved the most?

Elisabeth had the longest walk from her apartment on

M.

Poesie

As now in the land of childhood
The bond of friendship embraces us.
So also in later years
Let's share our joys and fears.

In friendly remembrance

Your friend Elisabeth
Berlin, April 4, 1935

RENI 1938

Schiller Strasse in Charlottenburg. Reni used to wait for her in front of her apartment on Eisenzahn Strasse, and I would be on the lookout for a sturdy short-haired Elisabeth and a thin Reni with light-brown braids, to join them for the last five-minute walk to school. I never admitted, even to myself, how jealous I was of their walk together before they met at my corner of Ravensberger and Eisenzahn. On the way home, I felt equally short-changed. Phone calls and occasional after-school meetings would momentarily abate my restlessness.

Occasionally I would get annoyed with Elisabeth's dogmatic opinions on books, movies and people. Winning a point meant a great deal to her. She never failed to underscore her victory with a self-righteous I-told-you-so. The less opinionated Reni would take the role of arbitrator in our arguments. Magnanimously, we would often let Elisabeth have her victories, with a look at each other that said, "Here she goes again."

Nevertheless, my feelings for Elisabeth were more

complex. We demanded more of one another and therefore were often disappointed. Our conflictual relationship created feelings of competition and envy. I envied Elisabeth the ease with which she related to the girls in our class and the way she was unfailingly tuned into their special needs.

Yet, these were momentary clouds in our friendship. We agreed more than we disagreed. We abhorred kitsch, we loathed small-talk, phonies, frills, affectations and crudeness. We admired elegance, beauty and poetry. Together we were growing up, creating ourselves.

As my mother and I neared our destination, I knew that the week's tragedies cancelled out all our squabbles and misunderstandings. This time our parting was not the result of anger, or momentary hurt feelings of neglect. This was real, caused by events beyond our control.

We had arranged to meet at the gate of our Schrebergarten. Most German cities had these small plots of land. They were named after Daniel Schreber, who, early in the nineteenth century, had introduced the idea of creating islands of repose, so that city dwellers could relax and plant a garden in the midst of encroaching urban growth.

In that little garden, off the beaten track, in the center of Berlin, our trio had spent many hot summer afternoons loafing, playing and talking. It seemed only natural to gather there this time.

While punctuality never was our greatest virtue, this time we three, accompanied by our mothers, arrived promptly. The mothers' handshakes were perfunctory and stiff. We girls looked at one another awkwardly. My mother handed me the key to open the rusty gate that enclosed the six-acre area, divided into twenty family plots. Two steps up, and the six of us filed along an uneven, narrow path with exposed tree roots. Arriving at our plot, I then opened the lock and lifted the chain that was coiled around the warped gate post.

Leaves covered the strawberry beds on the left and the

currant and gooseberry bushes on the right. We made our way along a short, overgrown path to a small, dilapidated shack that in the summers of our childhood stored garden furniture, toys and tools, and served as shelter from summer rains. The bleakness of the tarred roof, now full of cracks and holes, and the benches along the splintery latticed siding hardly reflected the warmth and joy of our lazy, sunny summer days. But on this afternoon, the plot was a safe enough place to meet. No one ever came here during the winter months.

Only with the coming of spring did life in the Schrebergarten resume as each leaseholder put his plot to its use according to preference. Our neighbors to the left, an unfriendly couple with two blond, skinny children, raised fruit and vegetables with a vengeance. They yelled at one another continually, and commanded their children to fetch water from the pump, to get on with their weeding, or to do their homework.

"And don't let us catch you talking to those Jews next door," they would call after them.

On the right, the Bernheims, a family much like ours, leased their plot so that their governess could take the children to a place more private than the Preussen Park across the street. Their grass was always immaculately cut, while ours looked like a wild meadow. Herr Bernheim, father of the twins Cary and Ralph, was an enthusiastic gardener, and spent his evenings and Sundays tending the lawn and flower beds. An Orthodox Jew, he spent Saturdays faithfully in the synagogue. On the Sabbath, when lighting candles, they always proclaimed *Mutti, lebe hoch* (hurrah for Mother), which struck me as mildly ridiculous.

When our own grass grew too much out of control, Fräulein Herta would borrow a neighbor's shears and clip an area large enough to make room for our garden chairs. When I became inspired to weed the straggly strawberry plants, Reni and Elisabeth, whose families were equally disinterested in gardening, occasionally helped with this unaccustomed task.

Reni, Elisabeth and I had been best friends during most of our lyzeum life. Our parents, however, were not part of that friendship. They hardly knew one another, had a different circle of friends, and different interests.

Elisabeth and her family had moved to Berlin from Mannheim, in southern Germany, when her father was forced to sell his department store. In 1934, Jews in southern Germany were already forbidden to own businesses. My most vivid recollections of Herr Arendt was his intimidating height, his booming voice, his raven-black hair and strong opinions, much like Elisabeth's. I don't believe that he ever again worked in Berlin. On my occasional visits, he seemed like a caged animal. He made nervous appearances to greet his daughter's guests and then vanished to the confines of his study. He impressed me as a deep thinker who should have been a scholar rather than a businessman.

Reni's father was headmaster of the prestigious French Gymnasium for boys, which had been founded by Huguenots in the eighteenth century. In hazy outlines, I remember a gentle, soft-spoken man with sandy hair. Although courteous and polite, he seemed to take very little interest in the girlfriends of his daughter. My father did not differ greatly in that respect. He must have been as puzzling to my two friends as their fathers were to me. Besides, he was rarely at home.

Our fathers had little enough in common; our mothers had even less. On this dreary afternoon, this unlikely group, so different in background, personality and looks, huddled uncomfortably on the hard and damp benches, at a loss for words. Face to face were Reni's short, reticent mother; Elisabeth's mother, who was graceful and spry; and my own mother, to me so humorless, embarrassed and stiff.

Reni's mother was a solid, stocky woman with a broad face and a narrow forehead that made her pointed nose look even more prominent. Her brownish hair gathered in a severe bun and her colorless gray coat made me think of a nun. Judging from the way her steel-blue eyes looked disapprovingly through me, I didn't think she liked me.

It was Elisabeth's mother who turned this awkward encounter into something bearable. She was the complete antithesis of the two other mothers. I had always envied Elisabeth her youthful and attractive mother who, despite obvious reversals in life-style, had retained her optimism and infectious gaiety. The sparkle in her eyes said all was well with the world.

She never failed to show her delight in welcoming Reni and me on our visits. At Elisabeth's apartment, we baked cookies, sewed costumes for the interminable plays we put on, or wrote poems. In Frau Arendt's presence, everything seemed within reach. She awakened us to fresh thoughts and, unlike my mother, never plagued us with irrelevant questions. She made us feel clever; when I was with her, I

MARIANNE, RENI AND ELISABETH (RIGHT) IN COSTUME FOR A PLAY — APRIL 1938

actually liked myself.

"So you are leaving tomorrow, Marianne," she said, with her unique southern German intonation. "How lucky. But we'll miss you."

The ice was broken. My mother proceeded to talk about our impending departure for Holland and our ultimate plans to follow Onkel Herman to Oregon.

"We, too, hope to leave soon," volunteered Reni's mother. "Friends are searching for a position of headmaster for my husband in England. We are waiting to hear."

Reni gaped amazed. She had not been told. Yet that did not surprise me. Her parents often kept things from her. When I had called to talk about us being expelled from school, she neither knew nor believed it. "This won't apply to me since I'm only half-Jewish," she had said. But it turned out to be only too true.

"I, too, want to leave," Frau Arendt joined in. "We have relatives in South America. But my husband is convinced that Hitler won't last. So we are staying."

Relieved that our mothers had connected, we announced that we would go for a short walk. Free once more, we took deep breaths and ran. Leaving the confines of our own garden, we scampered along the winding path that bordered the neighboring plots, with their private, securely padlocked fences. In the dusk of this chilly afternoon, they all looked neglected and abandoned.

After our sprint up and down the garden path, the three of us, as if drawn by a magnet, gravitated to the hollowed-out spot by the hawthorn hedge where, over the past summers, we regularly spied on our mystery garden.

"Remember the time they kissed," Reni said, "and the way they held each other close?"

On summer afternoons, the garden was filled with young people, eating, drinking, dancing, talking, and laughing, who seemed totally at ease in this kind of gathering. To us, it was like watching theatre on a beautiful stage set. The well-maintained lawn bordered a carefully trimmed bed of white and red geraniums, which in turn framed a small green pavilion with white trim. In the evenings, multi-colored lanterns accentuated the fairy-tale quality, while tango and fox-trot rhythms filled the air.

We reminisced about the spectacle we had often longingly watched through our opening in the hedge. Would we ever grow up to be as attractive and uninhibited? Some mysterious adult quality seemed present that we didn't quite understand. Yet, we were fascinated.

Elisabeth surprised us with her question. "It's true, isn't it? None of us has ever been kissed!" Her probing brown eyes looked for confirmation.

"Of course, you would have known," we assured her.

For once, we both felt impelled to lie. I knew that Reni's favorite cousin, who occasionally took her to a ballet or opera, had given her a kiss one night on the way home.

The previous December, I had been invited by Herr Stein, a family friend, to join him, his daughter Uschi, and his two sons for a skiing vacation in Czechoslovakia. My long-time casual friendship with Uschi could in no way compare in depth and intensity to the one I had with Reni and Elisabeth. Yet, she was good-natured and witty, and certainly would be a pleasant traveling companion. I felt lucky to be included in this winter-time adventure.

That year, knickers were in fashion. I had a smart navy-blue ski outfit with white gaiters that accentuated the knickers and the matching leather yoke on my belted jacket. I was trim and athletic. I had even earned the approval of my Nazi classmates for whom athletic achievement was a high priority. I did not share Uschi's fear of skiing. I loved it.

Uschi's brother Bruno, an ungainly and sulky fellow of seventeen, never so much as looked at me or uttered a word the entire trip. His dashing twenty-year-old brother Eric, however, was a striking contrast. Late one afternoon, returning from a horse-drawn sled ride through the snowy countryside, I rushed up to the warmth of the blue-and-white tiled stove in my room. A breathless Eric followed right behind. When we had been under the sled's heavy fur blankets, his hands had already begun to explore my legs and thighs. Now he pressed me against the welcoming tiled stove and began to kiss me, his lips still cold from our ride. To my joyful relief and Eric's great embarrassment, a puffy Herr Stein appeared at the room's threshold, short-circuiting any further amorous pursuits of his son.

Eric kept a sheepish distance from me for the remainder of the trip, checking out the local hotel bars for more appropriate female companions.

This startling episode remained my secret, as did my crush on Gabor, one of two young boys from Prague who

MARIANNE AT THE
TATRA LOMNITZ IN
CZECHOSLOVAKIA,
DECEMBER 1937

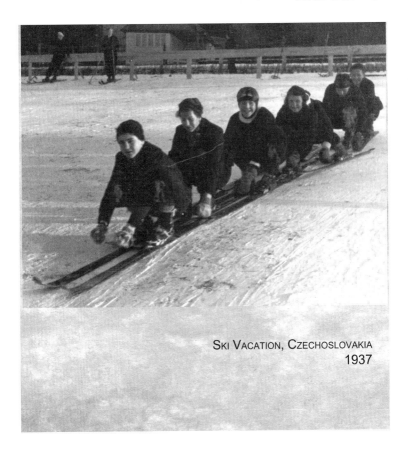

SKI VACATION, CZECHOSLOVAKIA
1937

were staying in our hotel. With them, Uschi and I explored ski trails and climbed steep hills so as to have the thrill of exhilarating down-hill runs later. Ski lifts were unknown, and we climbed with otter skins to keep from slipping.

With other kids our age, we organized slalom and downhill races. The greatest fun was the snake descent, with the skier in the lead holding the tips of the skis of the person in back, who in turn did the same. Sometimes as many as ten of us slid down the mountain, locked together in one configuration, to the applause of onlookers.

On the last night of our stay, Gabor walked me back to our hotel, a short distance from the restaurant. I still remember that strange feeling of tension and excitement. For the first time in my life, I was holding hands with a boy and I liked it. Everything about Gabor delighted me. He was an excellent skier. His well-chiseled features and high cheekbones reminded me of some movie star. At that time, I liked boys with curly hair. He told excellent jokes, had a wonderful laugh, and was great fun. The icy air of the Tatra mountains, the clear, star-studded sky, the sparkling, crunchy snow under our feet, all set the stage for that first welcome kiss.

This special moment remained my secret as well. I had, however, treated Reni and Elisabeth to detailed descriptions of skiing on the slopes of the Tatra mountains, the gripping cold, the afternoon tea dances to the sounds of the gypsy orchestra, and the delicious pastries. I reported on the heavy goulash dinners with dumplings and sour cream, and the generally relaxed and joyous atmosphere.

A festive air had also prevailed at two previous family skiing vacations the winter of 1936 at Keilberg, Czechoslovakia. We were joined by my father's piano-playing cousin Greta, her good-looking son Walter and his petite cousin Annemie. My pre-teen crush was totally ignored by the beautiful Walter, who was exceptionally attentive to Annemie!

It was so different from the now oppressive Germany. Sitting close in our small hollowed-out garden spot, each with our own thoughts, we started to feel the cold, and a novel kind of strain set in. We were coming to the end of a shared history.

"Let's go to the Preussen Park and see what's going on there," suggested Reni. "It'll just be for a minute. No one will bother us."

In the past, one of the main reasons for going to the park, diagonally across from the Schrebergarten, was to buy licorice

AN EARLIER SKIING VACATION WITH JULIAN, COUSIN WALTER (GRETA'S SON), AND HIS COUSIN ANNEMIE AT KEILBERG IN CZECHOSLOVAKIA, WINTER 1936

rolls at the candy kiosk or to play marbles. It was a meeting place for all the neighborhood kids, and we could always find a partner for marbles. I had become quite expert and had accumulated bags full of beautiful aggies of fine-grained quartz, peppermint stripes, immies, or scrap glass. The game's object was to shoot the marbles into a designated hole and to win the opponent's marbles, by knocking against them on the way to the hole. The newly acquired marble was for keeps, and we went in for heavy trading to increase our collections.

When not playing marbles, we visited the Preussen Park's adjacent ball field to fly kites. On spring and autumn weekends, the sky above was speckled with colorful moving objects of various sizes, their tails wiggling in the breeze, and young and old on terra firma manipulating their magic strings.

Marbles, kites and licorice kiosks were nowhere in sight this Friday afternoon. A few scattered couples in heavy winter coats walked briskly on the path that circled the large lawn area where, during the summer months, people crowded on benches. Today, those benches sat desolate and empty. Some children played ball, or hide-and-go-seek. For them, unlike for us, it was just another ordinary autumn afternoon.

"Let's quickly run around the circle one more time," I suggested. "Who will be first?"

We ran by the benches, the leaf-covered rose beds, the paths that radiated from the central square, where in our past summer games we would burst through bushes and around corners upon sweethearts in tender embrace or, much to our horror, upon a man exposing himself.

Breathless, with Reni and Elisabeth closely following, I was first to return to the candy kiosk, sealed off for the winter.

"Let's be sure to write, and let's tell each other everything." said Reni. We swore that we would.

For one last time, I looked at the faces of my two long-time friends. Our eyes met, and although sentimentality always had been something to avoid, we three hugged in a close circle and then, like birds, flew apart, and raced back to the garden gate, where our anxious mothers were pacing back and forth.

Benutzt die Luftpost!

BRÜCKLA... 16.7.7 1929 ... TRIESENBERG

Deutsches Reich

Standesamt Triberg

Vorgelesen, genehmigt und unterschr...

Julian S c h y b i l s k i

Erna S c h y b i l s k i , geb...

Herrmann Loewenberg,   Ale...

T he last two days merge into one. It seems as if the Baroness has just swept into our apartment and my father is still riding the subway. The relentless unfolding of events has speeded our departure, and Saturday, November 12, is our last night in Berlin.

MARIANNE'S LAST REPORT CARD FROM THE LYZEUM, 1938

Following our farewells in the Schrebergarten, the squeaky elevator deposits my mother and me for one last time at the door of the leased flat, which, devoid of memories or personal belongings, has demanded neither love nor attachment. It has served as the perfect vehicle for distancing myself from my Berlin childhood, and as a bridge to our new life.

Since my expulsion from the Lyzeum, my daily routine has been eclipsed. How would I spend my days? What would I do with myself? Oddly enough, being cut off from school has affected me less than seeing the van with all our belongings disappear in the distance, or gazing once more at the windows of our once-familiar former apartment, which now stared back at me ghost-like in its emptiness.

It is to my parents' credit that my dismissal from school turned into a painless, and even pleasant, episode.

"Don't worry, Mariannchen; you'll keep yourself busy," my mother had said. "You can read all you want; you can even do the cooking for us. And we'll take English lessons together."

Originally, we planned to stay in the temporary flat until our departure on the *Normandie* from Le Havre the end of January, 1939. I had feared four months of boredom and restlessness. However, our precipitous departure from Berlin, as well as a surprising transformation on the part of my mother, evaporated these fears.

Lacking the obliging presence of Else, Anna or Fräulein Herta, my mother has no choice but to tackle the household chores herself. Surprise! She gets up early and makes us all breakfast; she is cheerful, competent and chatty. For the first time in her life, she does not have to act the part of mistress of the house. Alone with the three of us, in the undemanding setting of the rented flat, she is not required to be cordial, to instruct the maids, or to show polite attention to Tante Toni. Liberated from constraints ingrained since early childhood, she leaves her bed unmade, scatters shoes and newspapers around, just as Tante Toni did, burns vegetables and overcooks meat. She knows that none of us holds these flaws against her. We admire her spirit and laugh together at the occasional mishaps. I am drawn to her by the twinkle in her

ERNA AND MARIANNE ON THE TERRACE AWAITING THE MOVERS, 1938

eyes and she in turn has begun to enjoy spending time with me. We talk, joke, play games and try our fractured English out on one another. We fantasize about life in America. Slowly, my mother's remoteness and changing moods erode. Even her intestinal maladies subside somewhat.

My mother talks with enthusiasm about our upcoming life with new people and new experiences. She does not want to repeat the past. And life will be different. Money will be tight, since all available funds will have to serve my father's business explorations. There will be no maids, and it is taken for granted that every one of us will have a hand in running the household. Will a simpler life, one with fewer obligations, better suit my mother's reserved nature and reveal previously hidden qualities?

My father is always home now. In shirt sleeves and without a tie, he lavishes much attention on my mother and infects her with his usual good humor. She has found a new serenity.

I, too, am changing. After my parting with Reni and Elisabeth, I begin to feel separated from the past, ready to leave. A tomorrow, with its yet unknown possibilities, awaits me, and for some unknown reason I feel optimistic about that future. The good phantoms of my past, the Baroness, Edith Margraf and Fräulein Herta, will accompany me.

The tightly drawn curtains reflect the lights from the dim table lamps and lend unreality to our last night. Our luggage stands ready in the hall. Only a few last-minute articles have yet to be added the following morning to the elegant small travel bag whose striking brown and orange plaid sides and solid leather grip is indeed worthy of a crossing on the *Normandie*. Our American visa has as yet not arrived, but we are confident that it will be issued in time for our scheduled crossing.

Sounds of crackling branches and passing cars seep in

Outings with the Löwenbergs from Görlitz. Left: Hans, Gerhard, Eveline and Marianne in the Riesengebirge with Rübezahl, a mythical forest spirit, 1933. Right: Ferry ride in the Spreewald, 1934.

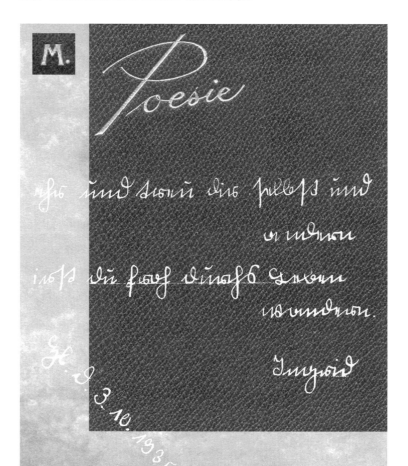

BE TRUE AND FAITHFUL TO YOURSELF AND OTHERS
THUS YOU'LL TRAVEL THROUGH LIFE WITH LITTLE HAZARD.

IN REMEMBRANCE

INGRID
OCTOBER 3, 1935

from the outside, as we gather once more around the table for a final meal. My father uncorks a bottle of red wine and Tante Toni, who has moved to an apartment close by, has brought supper consisting of Westphalian ham and salami sandwiches, with sour pickles from the Spreewald.

"Remember the last time we went to the Spreewald together," she says, straining to appear lighthearted. "Kurt was still alive. We floated down the Spree with the Löwenbergs and the Silbersteins."

I was ten at the time of that last annual get-together with the Görlitz contingent in the Spreewald, half-way between Berlin and Görlitz. Rybzek, who drove us that day, was a general factotum for Silberstein and Schybilski. He was a short, witty, arrogant Berliner, to whom nothing was sacred. His criticism of everyone and everything both amused and enraged my father to the degree that he occasionally fired him for his impertinence. But never for long. He missed his *Berliner Fresse* and hired him back.

For our Spreewald outing, Rybzek squeezed us into our black 1934 Buick and, with my father next to him giving driving orders or whistling, sped us to our rendezvous in Lübbenau, the small town on the Spree.

The Spreewald was famous for its salt pickles that had been marinated in enormous weathered vats and whose prominent presence in the village square served as a magnet. With large wooden prongs, the vendors fished the pickles out of their foamy, smelly brine, and for ten pfennigs handed them in a piece of newspaper to their impatient customers. Music, water, boats, picnics and pickles all mingle in my memory, with the shimmering folk costumes worn by the local inhabitants. Women in velvet skirts with colorful aprons, puffy blouses, and towering, starched white headdresses that looked like giant butterflies paraded about among us visitors. Our little group stuck closely together as we caught up with family news, walked, ate and floated up

Folk costumes on parade at The Spreewald 1930

and down the Spree on large boats before once more making our farewells and departing in opposite directions.

My father adds a drop of wine to my water, a special treat. We clink glasses, bite into the crunchy pickles and talk about happy family outings of the past, which briefly eclipse the sadness of leaving Tante Toni. Still no news from Fritz!

Deep in thought, my father stares into space. "Yes, I remember Silberstein on that trip. As usual, he made his caustic remarks." During their nearly fifteen years as business partners, my father had made valiant efforts to deal with the many problems that arose from their differences in personality. He had to forever counteract Alfred Silberstein's negative and defeatist attitudes and exert great energy to keep things from stagnating. "And can you imagine, he wants to follow us to Oregon and again go into business with me. They even decided to leave with us on tomorrow's plane, but it was all booked."

My mother is keeping quiet. The many years of the partnership had left their scars on her as well. She had resented the Silbersteins' ostentatiousness, freshly cut flowers on their table, summer and winter alike, extravagant dinner parties, Gretchen's flirtations with my father, her deviousness. "But you made it clear, Julchen," she interjects, "the next business venture you'll do on your own. I thought they are going to California."

"By all means, I don't want Peter around either," I add.

With this issue settled, everyone gets up from the table. Time to go to bed now! My mother looks pale and wan. The rings under her eyes are new. Is the tension of leaving catching up with her? We need to be up at six in the morning.

Sleep won't come. My mind races. My mother's worried look makes me face up to my own fear, which I have tried to keep hidden. I begin to worry that something could still get in the way of our safe departure. A bygone scary encounter with two S.A. men flashes through my mind. Onkel Benno had come to Berlin for the 1936 Olympics and invited my mother, my brother, and me to watch Jesse Owens run. All excited, we took the special S-Bahn from the Zoo Station that took us directly to the stadium where mobs of visitors pushed their way towards the arena. We had passed the gate, and were admiring the flags of the many participating nations when two lanky storm troopers in their avocado-brown uniforms demanded to see our tickets. My mother stares at the men frightened and bewildered. "My brother-in-law has them. He invited us and came all the way from America."

Onkel Benno 1935

But Onkel Benno is nowhere in sight and, in this steaming crowd, little chance exists of finding him.

"You want us to believe that?" The two blond men looked cynically at us and asked us if we were Jewish. "It figures, you tried to make your way in to watch a Negro. Well, you won't get to see him unless you produce those tickets."

Helpless, we looked around for Onkel Benno. We clutched my mother's arm for support, not knowing what these two men would do to us. A policeman joined our little group. Soon, people passing by gave us curious looks. The entire episode lasted no more than five minutes, but seemed like hours. Finally, our slim, bespattered Onkel in a gray suit and a gray hat appeared out of the crowd, looking anxious. For once he was neither smiling, chewing gum nor chomping on a cigar.

"There he is," cried my mother. The tickets were displayed. Reluctantly, they let us go.

The great event of Jesse Owens' victory was lost on us. Our seats were right in the center, across from the rostrum reserved for Hitler and other dignitaries of the Third Reich. But on that day, none of them were present.

I must have finally fallen off to sleep because the next thing I hear is my mother's voice telling me to get ready. The taxi will be here in half an hour.

For a last time, I get dressed in this Berlin room. I slip on the blue dress that matches my new peacock-blue coat, put on my socks, and tie my gray suede shoes.

The luggage is in the corridor outside our second-floor apartment. As we hear the elevator grind its way up, two pasty-faced, expressionless men with sandy hair and dark coats suddenly appear on the landing. My heart misses a beat. What brings them here on this quiet Sunday morning? Are they Gestapo, destined to snatch us before we escape? I sense everyone's paralysis. My father keeps going, opens the elevator door, and piles in the suitcases.

The two men in black, like two ghosts, pass silently behind us and climb the stairs to the next floor. My father loads the luggage in the elevator and descends with it. The rest of us rush down the stairs as if trying to escape everything evil, and fling ourselves into the waiting taxi.

Was it a real or an imagined danger? We shall never know. The two men were either SS in civilian clothes, rounding up Jews, but decided to let us go, or they were innocuous visitors of upstairs neighbors.

Tante Toni, who has brought the cab, escorts us to Tempelhof, the Berlin airport. With her usual good humor, she reassures us that we will be reunited soon. Fritz is on the verge of sending the papers. In the meantime, she will send anything we may still need to us in Holland.

No further unforeseen obstacles now interfere with our departure. Yet my parting from my aunt tears me apart, and shatters my composure. I have a premonition that I may never see her again. Hugging her, I have to be wrenched away by my parents to follow them and my little brother through the passport control and onto the plane.

"A pretty girl like you musn't cry," smiles a dashing young pilot who is helping passengers board the plane. What does he know about sadness, parting and loss?

From my airplane seat, I look out the small round window and see him waving at me. Timidly, my tears still streaming down my face, I return his smile and wave back, as gradually and with ceremonial dignity, the plane moves farther and farther away.

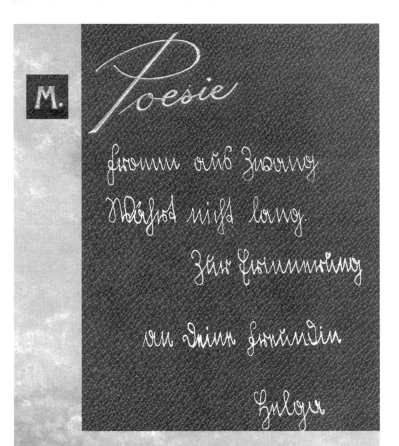

PIETY BY FORCE
DOES NOT ENDURE.
IN REMEMBRANCE OF

YOUR FRIEND, HELGA
OCTOBER 20, 1934

EPILOGUE

TANTE TONI DIED IN THE LITMANSTADT CONCENTRATION CAMP IN 1940.

RENI AND HER FAMILY LEFT FOR ENGLAND IN 1940, WHERE HER FATHER BECAME HEADMASTER OF A BOARDING SCHOOL.

ELISABETH AND HER FAMILY LIVED IN HIDING IN BERLIN THROUGHOUT THE WAR. THEY MOVED TO THE UNITED STATES IN 1946.

ONKEL MARTIN DIED OF BLOOD POISONING FROM AN INJECTION IN BERLIN IN 1938. TANTE ROSEL AND HER DAUGHTER STEFFI WERE DEPORTED TO THE RIGA GHETTO IN 1941 AND LATER WERE INTERNED IN A LATVIAN CONCENTRATION CAMP. THEY WERE LIBERATED BY THE INTERVENTION OF COUNT VON BERNADOTTE IN 1944. IN 1946, THEY WERE REUNITED IN SWEDEN, AND RELOCATED TO NEWARK, NEW JERSEY, WHERE THEY ESTABLISHED ANOTHER SUCCESSFUL CUSTOM QUILTING BUSINESS. STEFFI'S SISTER, HANNAH, HAD ESCAPED TO BELGIUM AND THEN FOLLOWED HER FAMILY TO NEWARK AFTER THE WAR. HANNAH RETURNED TO BERLIN WHERE SHE DIED IN 1987.

MY YOUNG COUSIN RUDI FROM DRESDEN, WHO HAD MOVED TO HOLLAND, PERISHED WITH HIS FAMILY IN AUSCHWITZ.

MY PIANO TEACHER, EDITH MARGRAF, AND HER HUSBAND WERE KILLED IN AUSCHWITZ.

THE SILBERSTEIN FAMILY LEFT FOR AMSTERDAM THE DAY AFTER OUR DEPARTURE. THEIR PLANE CRASHED UPON ARRIVAL. THEY WERE HOSPITALIZED FOR MINOR INJURIES. UPON RECOVERY, THEY WERE OBLIGED TO RETURN TO GERMANY FOR LACK OF A DUTCH ENTRANCE VISA. THEY ULTIMATELY ARRIVED IN LOS ANGELES IN THE WINTER OF 1940 AFTER A BRIEF STAY IN ENGLAND.

ARTUR AND HERTA MEYER EMIGRATED TO THE UNITED STATES AND SETTLED IN ST. LOUIS, MISSOURI, WHERE THEY LAUNCHED A CANDY BUSINESS THAT FLOURISHED. TANTE ROSA, HERTA'S MOTHER, JOINED THEM IN 1943, HAVING MADE THE TRIP THROUGH CHINA.

JULIUS BROH, VALLI'S WIDOWER, EMIGRATED TO THE UNITED STATES WITH HIS SON FRITZ AND ACQUIRED A HARDWARE STORE. ERICH, THE OTHER SON, EMIGRATED TO ARGENTINA AND BECAME THE OWNER OF A PAINT FACTORY.

MO AND KÄTE EISEMAN (TANTE ROSA'S DAUGHTER AND SON-IN-LAW) EMIGRATED TO THE UNITED STATES AND JOINED RELATIVES IN NEW JERSEY WHERE MO RAPIDLY FOUND EMPLOYMENT AS A CHEMIST.

MY FATHER'S COUSIN, GRETA FROM CHEMNITZ, WAS KILLED IN AUSCHWITZ.

MY MOTHER'S CHILDHOOD FRIEND, HILDE KAMM AND HER FAMILY WERE PART OF A GROUP ESCORTED TO SWITZERLAND IN

September, 1942, under the auspices of *Unternehmen Sieben* (Action Seven) spearheaded by Hans von Dohnanyi, Hans Oster and Wilhelm Canaris. These three honorable men were subsequently murdered by the Nazis.

Ruth, my friend from summer camp, emigrated to the United States instead of to England. Sara, Steffi and Gaby went to Israel, as planned.

Herr Hummel remained in Germany only until 1945. Disillusioned, he returned to Portland, Oregon.

Our family arrived safely in Holland. Lacking appropriate immigration papers, however, we also would have been returned to Germany on the next plane had my mother not suffered a severe intestinal attack. We were granted temporary asylum until our scheduled departure to the United States at the end of January, 1939.

The Hohenzollern Lyzeum changed its name twice. Hitler renamed it Königin Mathilde Schule. Its current name is Otto-von-Güericke Oberschule.

Numerous attempts to find traces of Baroness von Ameluxen remained unsuccessful.

ABOUT THE *POESIE ALBUM* . . .

P roverbs, poems and personal remembrances from friends, classmates and teachers fill the pages of young Marianne Schybilski's *Poesie Album* from March 1934 to April 1937. The six-inch square leather-bound book reflects the changing mood of Berliners during this time.